50 FASHION DESIGNERS

YOU SHOULD KNOW

50 FASHION DESIGNERS
YOU SHOULD KNOW

Simone Werle

Prestel

Munich · Berlin · London · New York

Front cover: Yasmeen Ghauri, Christian Dior, fall/winter 1997/98 © Nick Knight. Courtesy of Trunk Archive
Frontispiece: A creation by Tom Ford, Courtesy of Tom Ford
page 10/11: Creation of Calvin Klein at the Calvin Klein show 2004

© Prestel Verlag, Munich · Berlin · London · New York 2010
Picture credits: see page 157

Prestel, a member of Verlagsgruppe Random House GmbH

Prestel would like to thank
gettyimages®
for their kind cooperation

Prestel Verlag
Königinstrasse 9
80539 Munich
Tel. +49 (0)89 24 29 08-300
Fax +49 (0)89 24 29 08-335

Prestel Publishing Ltd.
4 Bloomsbury Place
London WC1A 2QA
Tel. +44 (0)20 7323-5004
Fax +44 (0)20 7636-8004

Prestel Publishing
900 Broadway, Suite 603
New York, N.Y. 10003
Tel. +1 (212) 995-2720
Fax +1 (212) 995-2733

www.prestel.com

Prestel books are available worldwide. Please contact your nearest bookseller or one of the above addresses for information
concerning your local distributor.

The Library of Congress Control Number: 2009943149
Library of Congress Control Number is available; British Library Cataloguing-in-Publication Data: a catalogue record for this book
is available from the British Library; Deutsche Nationalbibliothek holds a record of this publication in the Deutsche Nationalbibliografie;
detailed bibliographical data can be found under: http://dnb.d-nb.de

Text: Simone Werle with Stephanie Neumann
Project direction: Julia Strysio
Translated from German: Christine Shuttleworth, London
Copyediting: Jonathan Fox, Barcelona
Cover and design concept: LIQUID, Agentur für Gestaltung, Augsburg
Layout and production: zwischenschritt, Rainald Schwarz, Munich
Picture research: Simone Werle, Reegan Köster, Katharina Reiter, Julia Strysio
Timeline: Larissa Spicker
Origination: Reproline Mediateam
Printed and bound: Druckerei Uhl GmbH & Co. KG, Radolfzell

FSC
Mixed Sources
Product group from well-managed
forests and other controlled sources
Cert no. GFA-COC-001526
www.fsc.org
© 1996 Forest Stewardship Council

Verlagsgruppe Random House FSC-DEU-0100
The FSC-certified Opuspraximatt paper in this book
is produced by Condat and delivered by Deutsche Papier.

Printed in Germany

ISBN 978-3-7913-4413-3

CONTENTS

12 JEANNE LANVIN

14 MADELEINE VIONNET

16 PAUL POIRET

18 NINA RICCI

20 GABRIELLE "COCO" CHANEL

24 MAIN BOCHER

26 ELSA SCHIAPARELLI

28 CRISTÓBAL BALENCIAGA

30 CHRISTIAN DIOR

34 EMILIO PUCCI

38 PIERRE BALMAIN

40 MISSONI

44 ANDRÉ COURRÈGES

46 HUBERT DE GIVENCHY

48 ROY HALSTON

50 OSCAR DE LA RENTA

52 VALENTINO GARAVANI

56 EMANUEL UNGARO

58 MARY QUANT

60 GIORGIO ARMANI

64 YVES SAINT LAURENT

68 ISSEY MIYAKE

70 KARL LAGERFELD

74 RALPH LAUREN

76 KENZO TAKADA

80 AZZEDINE ALAÏA

82 VIVIENNE WESTWOOD

86 CALVIN KLEIN

90 REI KAWAKUBO

92 YOHJI YAMAMOTO

94 JIL SANDER

96 GIANNI VERSACE

100 DIANE VON FURSTENBERG

102 THIERRY MUGLER

104 DONNA KARAN

106 MIUCCIA PRADA

110 FRANCO MOSCHINO

112 CHRISTIAN LACROIX

114 JEAN PAUL GAULTIER

118 HELMUT LANG

120 MARTIN MARGIELA

124 DRIES VAN NOTEN

128 DOLCE & GABBANA

132 JOHN GALLIANO

136 TOM FORD

138 MARC JACOBS

142 HEDI SLIMANE

144 ALEXANDER MCQUEEN

148 HUSSEIN CHALAYAN

152 STELLA MCCARTNEY

155 GLOSSARY

156 INDEX

157 PHOTO CREDITS

JEANNE LANVIN ════════════════════════════

CLAUDE DEBUSSY ════════════════════════════

MAURICE RAVEL ════════════════════════

1825 Opening of the Bolshoi
Theater in Moscow

1844 Silesian weavers' revolt

1858 Charles Frederick Worth opens the
first fashion shop in Paris

1871 Charles Darwin publishes
The Descent of Man

1889 Opening of the Moulin
Rouge in Paris

| 1815 | 1820 | 1825 | 1830 | 1835 | 1840 | 1845 | 1850 | 1855 | 1860 | 1865 | 1870 | 1875 | 1880 | 1885 | 1890 | 1895 | 1900 |

Black and white dress by Jeanne Lanvin,
1954

1922–53 Josef Stalin is general secretary of the
Communist Party of the Soviet Union

1956 Elvis Presley releases "Heartbreak
Hotel," his first big hit

1905 Founding of the artists' group
Die Brücke in Dresden

1937 Pablo Picasso paints *Guernica*

1971 Women given the vote in
Switzerland

1905   1910   1915   1920   1925   1930   1935   1940   1945   1950   1955   1960   1965   1970   1975   1980   1985   1990

JEANNE LANVIN

A long history of success: the Lanvin fashion house is the oldest in the world. The first creations by the later haute couture salon were simple clothes for children.

If one glances behind the imposing façade of Rue du Faubourg Saint-Honoré, 22, in Paris, one will see a world full of history. For this is the Lanvin headquarters, the oldest couture house in the world. Founded by Jeanne Lanvin, who at the outset of her career could not even afford to buy fabric for her creations.

Lanvin's first contact with fashion came early in life—admittedly less out of creative passion than economic hardship. In order to help support her six younger siblings, Lanvin, then only fifteen, took a job with a tailor in the suburbs of Paris. In 1890, at twenty-seven, Lanvin took the daring leap into independence, though on a modest scale. Not far from the splendid head office of today, she rented two rooms in which, for lack of fabric, she at first made only hats. Since the severe children's fashions of the turn of the century did not appeal to her, she tailored the clothing for her young daughter Marguerite herself: tunic dresses designed for easy movement (sans tight corsets or starched collars) in colorful patterned cotton fabrics, generally adorned with elaborate smocking. The gentle Marguerite, later known as Marie-Blanche, was to become the Salon Lanvin's first model. When walking on the street, other mothers asked Lanvin and her daughter from where the colorful loose dresses came. The result: a flood of commissions. Jeanne Lanvin had found her niche—and made use of her opportunity. With the help of a loan of 300 francs and the good will of her fabric suppliers, she launched her fashion lines "Enfant" and "Jeune Fille." The style of this junior haute couture (the first on sale in Paris) varied mainly in the choice of fabrics, the embroidery, and the colors. The silhouette meanwhile remained the same: a close-fitting top with a long, fluffy, flared skirt, set low on the hips. What is known today as a *robe de style* is the exclusive invention of the Parisian fashion pioneer. There soon followed women's haute couture, which beginning in the twenties was among the most distinguished in Paris. Her trademark was softly flowing fabrics, multilayered elegant cuts, and the bold use of color.

Lanvin prized contact with the artists and the creative youth who inspired her creations. To take full advantage of her first-class embroidery department, Lanvin, always highly efficient in business and organizational matters, launched her first men's collection in 1926. Its focus was on the richly embroidered official uniforms of the Académie Française.

With the death of its founder in 1946 the house experienced a series of changes in designer, including Lanvin's daughter Marie-Blanche (1946), Giorgio Armani (1989, see page 60), and Claude Montana (1990). But only Alber Elbaz (responsible for the women's collections since 2001) and Lucas Ossendrijver (responsible for the men's collections since 2006) were able to bring the label back among the top fashion houses.

1867 Born in Paris on January 1
1889 Opens a hat shop in Paris
1908 Adds children's clothes to the business
1909 Adds women's clothes to the business
1920 Introduces a home decorations line
1923 Building of a dye factory in Nanterre and introduction of a sportswear collection
1924 Opens fashion boutiques in Cannes and Le Touquet and a perfume shop in Paris
1925 Creation of her first perfume, My Sin
1926 Presents the first men's collection
1946 Dies in Paris on July 6

Jeanne Lanvin in Paris, 1900

1837 Louis Daguerre invents
the daguerreotype

1851 First issue of the
New York Times

1871 Giuseppe Verdi's opera *Aida*
premieres in Cairo

1897 Founding of the artists' group
the Vienna Secession

1825 1830 1835 1840 1845 1850 1855 1860 1865 1870 1875 1880 1885 1890 1895 1900 1905 1910

1936 Premiere of Charlie Chaplin's
film *Modern Times*

1957 Albert Camus awarded the
Nobel Prize for Literature

1989 Massacre in Beijing's
Tiananmen Square

1914–18 World War I

1946 Founding of UNESCO

1971 Jim Morrison dies in Paris

1915 1920 1925 1930 1935 1940 1945 1950 1955 1960 1965 1970 1975 1980 1985 1990 1995 2000

MADELEINE VIONNET

The French designer was the first to combine effortless elegance with natural comfort. She was known as the "Queen of the bias cut"—and yet she is now practically forgotten.

Diana Vreeland, for many years editor in chief of American *Vogue* and known for her acid pen, called her nothing less than the "most important fashion designer of the twentieth century." Azzedine Alaïa (see page 80) characterizes her as "the source of everything that lives on in our subconscious." And the legendary fashion journalist Suzy Menkes quite simply finds everything about her "utterly modern." One thing is certain: among connoisseurs of fashion, Madeleine Vionnet, member of the Paris haute couture scene of the interwar years, is considered the "mother of all couturiers." For everyone else, Vionnet the fashion pioneer is hardly more than a name long since forgotten. Unjustly, for her artistic influence is still very much in evidence.

Although the grand master of fashion, Paul Poiret (see page 16), claimed exclusive credit for getting rid of the corset, the young Vionnet was actually the first designer to banish the armor-like garment from her creations. At the start of the twentieth century, during her time with the fashion designer Jacques Doucet, Madeleine Vionnet designed feather-light, softly draped clothing distinguished not merely by the absence of a corset. The adoptive Parisian also forged entirely new paths in her handling of fabrics. Vionnet not only experimented with cuts (she was the first to work consistently with triangular inserts, circular cuts, vents, cowl necklines, and halter necks), but also, with her exceptional feel for form and pattern, raised women's couture to a whole new level. This fashion architect's most important innovation was the bias cut, in which the fabric is cut and worked, not as usual in parallel lines, but on the bias, at 45 degrees to the direction of the thread. This technique results in flattering clothes that flow softly around the body, following the wearer's movements and yet seeming to lead a fascinating life of their own. The symbiosis of body and clothes was in fact one of the most important principles in the work of this skilled couturier: "When a woman smiles, her dress must smile with her." In this context, it is not surprising to learn of her loathing of everything fashionable: "There is something superficial and volatile about the seasonal and elusive whims of fashion which offends my sense of beauty." And indeed, Vionnet's love of the Greek ideal of beauty decisively influenced her working methods.

Vionnet was fascinated by classical antiquity and its draperies. Her fashion house was adorned with frescoes showing Greek beauties wearing Vionnet designs. Inspired by the fall of the drapes in ancient Greek robes, she never created her designs as mere two-dimensional sketches on paper. Her "fashion illustrations" were models in simple course cloth, displayed on an eighty-centimeter-tall wooden doll. For the realization of her creations, however, she used more sophisticated fabrics such as *crêpe de chine*, charmeuse, and silk muslin.

In spite of it all, Madeleine Vionnet, perhaps the most gifted fashion designer of the twentieth century, has found only a supporting role in fashion's collective memory in comparison to her contemporaries Coco Chanel (see page 20) and Elsa Schiaparelli (see page 26). Vionnet may have discovered the perfect cut, but she understood comparatively little about crowd-pleasing self-promotion. Perhaps it was merely her reserved manner that ensured we know the clothes but not the woman who designed them. And so her legacy today remains visible—yet nameless.

1876 Born in Chilleurs-aux-Bois, France, on June 22
1888 Begins tailoring apprenticeship at age 12
1896–1901 Runs a tailoring business in London
1891–1906 Cutter and director of couture in the Callot Soeur fashion studio in Paris
1907–12 Director of couture at Jacques Doucet
1912 Opens her own salon in Paris
1923 Invents bias cutting
1940 Closes her salon after the outbreak of World War II and retires to a farm in Cély
1975 Dies in Paris on March 2

left page
Crêpe ensemble, ca. 1931

above
Madeleine Vionnet pinning a dress design, ca. 1930

1840 First portrait photography
studio in the U.S.

1861 Outbreak of the American
Civil War

1883–85 First skyscraper
constructed in Chicago

1900 Sigmund Freud publishes
The Interpretation of Dreams

| 1830 | 1835 | 1840 | 1845 | 1850 | 1855 | 1860 | 1865 | 1870 | 1875 | 1880 | 1885 | 1890 | 1895 | 1900 | 1905 | 1910 | 1915 |

Ensemble consisting of softly draped jacket
and pants, 1925

1929 Opening of the Museum of
Modern Art in New York

1959 Alaska and Hawaii become
the 49th and 50th U.S. states

1998 Founding of the
anti-globaliza-
tion network
Attac

1979 Soviet troops invade Afghanistan

1917 October Revolution in Russia

1947 UN partition plan for Palestine

1920   1925   1930   1935   1940   1945   1950   1955   1960   1965   1970   1975   1980   1985   1990   1995   2000   2005

PAUL POIRET

This French designer was the first great fashion revolutionary. His greatest achievement was the abolishment of the corset.

Every age has its own prophet—someone who knows the secret longings of his or her contemporaries and is capable of converting them into public demand. Paul Poiret, the Parisian fashion designer, was just such a visionary. His modern, corset-free silhouettes broke with everything considered to be fashionable before 1905. The Frenchman is still considered today one of the most innovative designers in the history of haute couture. Almost as legendary is his financial extravagance. He died in 1944 in abject poverty, a genius forgotten by the world.

As a teenager, Poiret, the son of a cloth merchant, was already selling fashion drawings and small designs to Paris fashion studios. After training with the couturiers Jacques Doucet and Charles Frederick Worth he finally went into business with his own salon in 1903. His muse was his young wife, Denise Boulet. Slim, emancipated, and independent, she was the perfect advertisement for Poiret's vision. At a time when the female body was still divided into protruding bosom and buttocks, Boulet's athletic figure served as a basis for Poiret's loosely hanging garments, draped directly on the body (he couldn't sew), and for whose fit neither hoop skirt nor corset was required.

Poiret's most daring designs included pants for women, which till then were only considered acceptable, if at all, for bicycling. His culotte skirts and harem pantaloons led to riots in the streets, sometimes even resulting in the arrest of their wearers. In 1911, the designer took a step backward, at least from the point of view of emancipation. With the design of the hobble skirt, he, having freed the female bosom, shackled the legs and thus the freedom of the wearer. Additional creations were "lampshade" tunics, T-shirt dresses, and the robe culotte, a kind of jumpsuit.

Above all, Poiret's designs were inspired by art and culture. When he presented his harem fashions, the stories of Scheherezade had just been translated into French. The Ballets Russes, visiting Paris in 1909, prompted his turbans, coats with kimono sleeves, richly decorated tunics, and flat slippers. His expressive color schemes seem to have been borrowed directly from the group of controversial artists known as the Fauves (the wild beasts). His models, mostly produced with the use of extravagantly gorgeous fabrics, are marked by an exciting contrast between impressive modernity and stunning theatricality.

Like no designer before him, Poiret had an infallible instinct for marketing. He traveled to Russia and the U.S. to present his creations in person (and pick up ideas for new designs). He complemented his fashions with perfume, makeup, nail polish, and interiors. Following the principle of the gesamtkunstwerk (total work of art), Poiret introduced the decorated window display and gave fashion photography, then still in its infancy, an artistic direction. His legendary Oriental banquets (at one of which half-naked, dusky waiters served 900 liters of champagne to 300 guests) are considered among the first modern PR stunts.

Poiret's style, derived from Art Deco, was considered groundbreaking until the end of World War I. After that, the eccentric designer increasingly began to lose his prosperous clientele to other ambitious designers, above all Jean Patou and Coco Chanel (see page 20). In 1925, with one last grand appearance, he sealed his own demise. Deep in debt, he rented three luxurious ships to present his collection at the Paris Arts Décoratifs show. Despite the expense, his competitors could not be fought off. In 1926 he left the fashion house he had founded, and in 1929 his wife and muse finally left him. Fifteen years later Poiret died a *clochard*, a homeless vagrant, in the occupied Paris of World War II.

1879 Born in Paris on April 20
1898–1903 Trains as a designer with Jacques Doucet and Charles Frederick Worth
1903 Opens haute couture salon in Paris
1910–11 Textile designs by Raoul Dufy
1911 Creates his first perfume, Rosine, and sets up a school for arts and crafts with a retail boutique
1912 Opens a studio for packaging design
1913 Presents his collections in New York
1914 Designs a military coat for the French army
1921–25 Opens several branches in France
1929 Insolvency of the fashion house
1944 Dies in Paris on April 28

Paul Poiret at a fitting, 1925

NINA RICCI ═══

MAURICE RAVEL ═══

MARLENE DIETRICH ═══════════════════════

1851 First World's Fair (the Great
Exhibition) in London

1897 Opening of the Tate Gallery
in London

1861 In Australia, women are
granted voting rights

1880 First electric elevator put into
operation in Mannheim, Germany

1912 Founding of the
Republic of China

1835	1840	1845	1850	1855	1860	1865	1870	1875	1880	1885	1890	1895	1900	1905	1910	1915	1920

Beaded dress, 1951

1928 Alexander Fleming
discovers penicillin

1945 Beginning of the Cold War

1959 Cuban Revolution

1980 Awarding of the first "Alternative
Nobel Prize" in Stockholm

1999 War in Kosovo

1925   1930   1935   1940   1945   1950   1955   1960   1965   1970   1975   1980   1985   1990   1995   2000   2005   2010

NINA RICCI

This French-Italian designer combined feminine romanticism with discreet sensuality.

To open an haute couture salon during a global economic crisis circa 1932 demanded two qualities above all: courage and experience. Nina Ricci had both. Her courage was steeled by son Robert, whose firm belief in his mother's skills persuaded Ricci to strike out on her own. As for experience, she had more than thirty years of it.

Ricci was born in Turin in 1883 and named Maria— Nina was her nickname. As a child she moved with her family to Florence, and as a teenager to Paris, where she entered into an apprenticeship as a seamstress. At only eighteen years of age she was promoted to manager of the salon, and at twenty-two she was given sole responsibility as designer. In 1908 Nina Ricci moved to a position as designer at the couture house of Raffin, whose business partner she was later to become. Her big leap followed in 1932, when at over fifty years of age she became independent, opening the House of Nina Ricci together with her son (who instigated the under-taking). The roles in this family business were clearly allocated according to talent: Robert, with his business acumen, took care of finances, and Nina, with her technical expertise and impeccable taste, was in charge of the style of the haute couture house.

Without the need for a preliminary sketch, like Madeleine Vionnet (see page 14) and Paul Poiret (see page 16), Nina Ricci worked with a light fabric placed directly on the body of the living model, after which the paper pattern was created. At a time when Elsa Schiaparelli (see page 26) was causing a scandal with her artistic extravagance, and Coco Chanel (see page 20) was transforming fashion with eye-popping sophistication, Nina Ricci's creations were one thing above all: exceptionally delightful. Not only for the wearer (the highest quality material and flawless craftsmanship were a must), but also and above all for the observer. Ricci's ensembles achieved a perfect harmony between girlish romanticism and discreet sensuality. Her masterly treatment of patterns remains legendary today (Ricci was even able to use checkered fabric on a bias cut). In other words, exactly the right thing for the crisis-shaken ladies of the Parisian upper classes.

Soon the house became a worldwide symbol of Parisian taste. Ricci, who had begun in 1932 with forty seamstresses, was able to increase that number tenfold in only five years. Thanks to Robert's skilful management, the house even survived the turmoil of World War II unscathed. And it was he who created the perfume L'Air du Temps, whose production marked the beginning of his partnership with the art deco artist Marc Lalique.

In 1954, Nina Ricci retired as chief designer at age seventy. On her death in 1970, the control of the house was first taken over by the designer Jules-François Crahay, who had already inherited the creative legacy of the couturiere. After several changes of designer, since 2009 Peter Copping (formerly at Louis Vuitton) has been responsible for the feminine, sophisticated image of the fashion house.

1883 Born in Turin on January 14
1895 Begins an apprenticeship in couture in Paris
1908–28 Fashion designer for the house of Raffin
1932 Founds her own fashion house in Paris with son Robert as business manager
1945 Takes part in a fashion show at the Louvre in Paris
1946 Robert Ricci creates the first perfume for the business, L'Air du Temps
1954 Retires as chief designer
1970 Dies in Paris on November 30

Maria Nielli, better known as Nina Ricci

COCO CHANEL

IGOR STRAVINSKY

JEAN COCTEAU

1848 Wave of revolutions
sweeps Europe

1877 Queen Victoria of the United Kingdom
takes the title of Empress of India

1865 Abolition of slavery in
the U.S.

1893 Edvard Munch paints *The Scream*

1912 The *Titanic* sinks in
the North Atlantic

1835 1840 1845 1850 1855 1860 1865 1870 1875 1880 1885 1890 1895 1900 1905 1910 1915 1920

1927 First transatlantic telephone call
from New York to London

1941 Premiere of Orson Welles' film
Citizen Kane

1957 Premiere of Leonard Bernstein's musical
West Side Story on Broadway

1976 Helmut Newton publishes his first
photography book, *White Women*

1997 Accidental death
of Diana, Princess
of Wales

| 1925 | 1930 | 1935 | 1940 | 1945 | 1950 | 1955 | 1960 | 1965 | 1970 | 1975 | 1980 | 1985 | 1990 | 1995 | 2000 | 2005 | 2010 |

GABRIELLE "COCO" CHANEL

She came from nowhere and died an icon. The designs of this influential couturier permanently changed the look of the modern woman.

Throughout her life she was always called "Mademoiselle," but in reality she was the grande dame of fashion. Gabrielle Chanel, known as Coco, invented the "little black dress," quilted handbags, the tweed suit, and, not least, the legendary logo consisting of an interlocking double-C. Her unpretentiously luxurious designs perfectly suited the female form, and her collections the spirit of a new generation.

Born in 1883 in impoverished circumstances, she grew up in the orphanage of a convent and rose in record time from a modest textile shopgirl and occasional chanteuse to a couture legend. With her numerous lovers, Chanel, who never married, had not only procured the starting capital for her later fashion empire, but above all learned through observation everything she needed for success in business: vision, discipline, strategic skill, and perseverance. She was the embodiment of the modern career woman long before they populated the metropolises of the world. And since she was her own favorite model, she actually designed for women who did not as yet exist.

With Chanel, women's liberation was consistently turned upside down: in 1910 she set herself up as a milliner in a lover's bachelor apartment, where she radically reworked ready-made hats of the belle époque. Three years later she opened a fashion salon in Deauville, another in Biarritz in 1915, and finally, in 1919, one on the Rue Cambon in Paris, still the headquarters of the house of Chanel. For Chanel, elegance meant nothing without comfort and simplicity. She therefore created her fashions against prevailing trends, making suits with large, unladylike patch pockets whose loose fit was matched only by the material used: soft cotton jersey, previously used only in the manufacture of men's underwear. She shortened the hems of skirts to a sensational length just below the knee, abandoned frills and flounces, and made costume

jewelry fashionable. No corset was needed for her sailor blouses, lightweight sweaters, ladies' pants, and youthful drop-waist tunic dresses. Even if she was not the first to renounce the constricting garment—Madeleine Vionnet (see page 14) and Paul Poiret (see page 16) had previously done so—it was she who ultimately banned the corset from the wardrobes of the world. As the attractive archetype of the modern woman, her approach to presenting her style to a society eager for change was highly personal. Chanel was not simply about fashion. Chanel was about a new way of life.

Like most of the haute couture houses, Chanel closed her doors during World War II. In 1954, at the age of seventy-one, out of boredom and blind rage, she finally dared to make her comeback. With his New Look, Christian Dior had revived an image of women that Coco Chanel thought she had banished decades earlier. Her weapons in the rekindled battle were tweed suits, quilted bags, and the famous "little black dress"—all bestsellers, which her successor Karl Lagerfeld (see page 70) consistently reinterprets. Up to the present day, Chanel's philosophy has not lost even the slightest bit of its modernity.

1883 Born in Saumur, France, on
      August 19 as Gabrielle Bonheur
      Chanel
1910 Opens a milliner's studio in Paris
1911 Opens her first fashion house in
      Paris
1921 Launch of the perfume Chanel
      No. 5
1924 Presents first costume jewelry
1926 Creation of the "little black
      dress"
1939 Closes her fashion house
1954 Re-opens business and makes a
      comeback with the tweed suit
1971 Dies in Paris on January 10

left page
Classic Chanel bouclé suit, 1960

above
Coco Chanel, ca. 1936

1848 Beginning of the California
Gold Rush

1865 Assassination of U.S. president
Abraham Lincoln

1885 Karl Benz builds the first automobile
with a gasoline engine

1909 Sergei Diaghilev founds the
Ballets Russes in Paris

1895 Oscar Wilde publishes *The Importance of Being Earnest*

1840 1845 1850 1855 1860 1865 1870 1875 1880 1885 1890 1895 1900 1905 1910 1915 1920 1925

Black satin ensemble consisting of gown,
fur-trimmed cape, and matching cap

1945 Founding of the Socialist Federal
Republic of Yugoslavia

1929 Ernest Hemingway publishes
A Farewell to Arms

1961 John F. Kennedy becomes
35th U.S. president

1979–89 Soviet invasion of Afghanistan

2001 Launch of the
Apple iPod

1930 1935 1940 1945 1950 1955 1960 1965 1970 1975 1980 1985 1990 1995 2000 2005 2010 2015

MAIN BOCHER

He was the first American designer to open a couture house in Paris. His fabulously expensive clothes were uncommonly simple for the 1930s.

"I've never done eccentric things. I've always made clothes for ladies." With his unique sense of discreet, timeless elegance, Main Bocher pulled off a double miracle in the thirties: he was not only the first American to open his own couture house in Paris, but he also managed to do so during the Depression. What should actually have been doomed to failure became a worldwide success. The couturier from Chicago with no formal training was such an unbelievable master of bias cutting that even his couture colleague, the designer Madeleine Vionnet (see page 14), was deeply impressed. His slender dresses flowed around the body in the most flattering fashion and, despite being made from the highest-quality silk fabrics, were almost outrageously simple for the time. Main Bocher, who enjoyed the reputation of being the most expensive couturier in the world, was not interested in mass production, but worked only on commission. His clothes continued to be made almost entirely by hand until the very end.

The miracle began in Paris. It was here that a then unknown American named Main Rousseau Bocher opened a fashion house in 1929—between two world wars, in the middle of the Depression, and in the heart of the elegant Avenue George V. After several years as an illustrator for *Harper's Bazaar* and later as editor of French *Vogue* he had learned so much about couture that he decided to switch sides—from fashion observer to fashion designer. He gave himself the sonorous name of Mainbocher and got started. This designer with bad timing had not only talent but also exceptional luck. Despite the economic crisis, this "exotic" character was supported from the beginning by his American compatriots, and more so their wives. Mainbocher stood out. Not only for his origins. Not only for his surprisingly simple evening gowns that were short rather than long, and that at times even appeared in peasant patterns. Main Bocher also stood out for

his high prices. Among his first fans was Wallis Simpson, later Duchess of Windsor. For her 1937 marriage to King Edward VIII (from then on the Duke of Windsor) she ordered a design from Mainbocher. He created a gown in silk crepe—high-necked, with a tie-cinched waist and floor-length, slender skirt. The wedding became a media event, and Mainbocher became world famous overnight. So famous that even World War II could not touch him. While Coco Chanel (see page 20) closed her studio, Main Bocher took his with him back to the U.S. New York was impatiently awaiting America's star couturier from Paris. At his first show in the fall of 1940 there was such a crowd that, as reported by the *New York Times*, some young women sat on the floor because there was not a single free chair. The name of Mainbocher became a fashion must among high society. In 1945, with the war just over, $1,000 could only buy a blouse, and there was not a single dress for less than $4,000.

Evening wear was Mainbocher's specialty. In the course of his forty-year career he created a number of variations on the classic black dress, at times draping a wrap jacket with a fur trimmed shawl collar over it, at times adding flowers or overskirts. It was not until the age of eighty that Main Bocher managed to separate himself from fashion. In 1971 he closed his salon, and from then on lived in Paris and Munich. He mourned the deaths of his friends and colleagues Cristóbal Balenciaga (see page 28) and Madeleine Vionnet. And he deplored what he saw as an alarming absence of taste in fashion. Until the very end the designer dreamed of a comeback to once again convince the world of the beauty of simple elegance.

1890 Born in Chicago on October 24
as Main Rousseau Bocher
1907–14 Studies art in Chicago,
New York, Munich, and Paris
1917–18 Military service in Paris
1917–21 Fashion illustrator for
Harper's Bazaar in Paris
1922–29 Fashion correspondent and
later editor of French *Vogue*
1929 Founds a fashion house in Paris
1940 Moves his business to New York
1942 Designs uniforms for the U.S.
Navy
1976 Dies on December 27

Main Bocher, in his forties

1848 Karl Marx and Friedrich Engels publish
The Communist Manifesto

1882 Robert Koch isolates the
tuberculosis bacillus

1919 German colon
in Africa taken
over by the U.
and France

1866 U.S. Civil Rights Act extends rights
of emancipated slaves

1891 Paul Gauguin's first journey
to Tahiti

1907 Pablo Picasso
paints *Les Demoi-
selles d'Avignon*

| 1840 | 1845 | 1850 | 1855 | 1860 | 1865 | 1870 | 1875 | 1880 | 1885 | 1890 | 1895 | 1900 | 1905 | 1910 | 1915 | 1920 | 1925 |

In 1937, Salvador Dalí's lobster inspired
Elsa Schiaparelli to design an evening
gown in painted silk etamine.

1933 Franklin D. Roosevelt becomes
32nd U.S. president

1963 Martin Luther King delivers his
"I have a dream" speech

1947 India wins independence from the United Kingdom

1981 First space shuttle flight (*Columbia*)

1930   1935   1940   1945   1950   1955   1960   1965   1970   1975   1980   1985   1990   1995   2000   2005   2010   2015

ELSA SCHIAPARELLI

The creations of this Italian designer were Surrealism transformed into fabric, blurring the border between art and fashion.

Her keenest rival, Coco Chanel, called her simply "this Italian artist who makes clothes." In contrast to Chanel (see page 20), the champion of functional elegance, Elsa Schiaparelli was the rare bird among Parisian couturiers and, at the same time, more than a mere fashion designer; her fantastic, sometimes audacious fabric structures today remain an impressive demonstration of what clothing looks like when art and fashion embrace.

Well-traveled (from Rome via London to Chicago and New York) and newly divorced, the Italian designer settled in Paris in 1922 with her daughter Gogo. Soon she was designing her first sweaters inspired by the artistic avant-garde to which she would soon belong. These motifs, knitted sailors' tattoos, neckties, and an outlined ribcage, were "shocking," quite in keeping with the motto she later chose for herself (from which her famous "shocking pink" was also later derived). These pieces were at first intended only for Schiaparelli's private use—until an American buyer discovered them and promptly ordered forty sweaters. Schiaparelli, who had never been trained as a designer (in Rome she studied philosophy), became overnight, at more than thirty years of age, a couturier. Two years later she was employing 400 staff members in eight studios. Her collections were scandalous pyrotechnic displays of textile creativity—as though specifically designed for the exuberant interwar period.

Schiaparelli's approach was never of a purely aesthetic nature. Fashion, as she wrote later, "is born by small facts, trends, or even politics, never by trying to make little pleats and furbelows, by trinkets, by clothes easy to copy, or by the shortening or lengthening of a skirt." And even if she changed the silhouette of her garments with every collection (retaining only the wide shoulders she created), and had no fear of unusual materials (she used glass fiber, latex, cellophane, and sackcloth),

it was the link with the world of art that defined her surreal collections.

Jean Cocteau sketched the sewing patterns for her fabrics and Pablo Picasso inspired her fabrics decorated with newsprint, while the oversized lobster on one of her evening gowns came from Salvador Dalí. Also with Dalí, "Schiap," as she was called, designed the famous telephone purse in black velvet with a gold dial. Speaking of accessories: she was one of the first fashion designs to create a whole range of gloves, jewelry, watches, shawls, bathing suits, and purses, all of which bore her label (although at the time this was still known unpretentiously as a "tag"). And it was particularly here that Elsa Schiaparelli showed her devastating wit: she had buttons made in the shape of padlocks, circus horses, and musical instruments, threaded aspirin tablets into bracelets, and allowed zippers to be clearly visible in her haute couture. Her hats were shaped like brains, inkwells with quills, or, relatively tamely, like the Eiffel Tower.

When the Germans marched into Paris, Schiaparelli immigrated to the U.S. After the war, back in the French capital, the creative fun was over. Christian Dior's New Look (see page 30) determined the style of the new age, and little space was left for Schiaparelli's fantastically extravagant creations. By 1954, the salon of this great artist of haute couture had become design history.

1890 Born in Rome on September 10
1928 Opens a studio in Paris, followed by a salon in London
1935 Takes over the fashion house of Chéruit under her own name
1936 Textile designs by Salvador Dalí
1937 Launch of her first perfume, Shocking
1939 Works with Jean Cocteau on fall collection
1940–45 Exile in New York
1949 Opens a branch in New York
1954 Final closure of the salon and retirement from the fashion business
1973 Dies in Paris on November 14

Elsa Schiaparelli with one of her own creations

1879 Thomas Alva Edison invents the
carbon-filament light bulb

1927 Charles Lindberg
crosses the
Atlantic on a
non-stop flight

1861–65 American Civil War

1895 First Venice Biennale

1910 The first film producers
settle in Hollywood

| 1845 | 1850 | 1855 | 1860 | 1865 | 1870 | 1875 | 1880 | 1885 | 1890 | 1895 | 1900 | 1905 | 1910 | 1915 | 1920 | 1925 | 1930 |

1961 First human in space (USSR)

1943 Premiere of *Casablanca*, directed
by Michael Curtiz

1991 Collapse of the USSR

1979 Margaret Thatcher becomes prime
minister of the United Kingdom

2001 Terrorist attacks in the U.S.
on September 11

| 1935 | 1940 | 1945 | 1950 | 1955 | 1960 | 1965 | 1970 | 1975 | 1980 | 1985 | 1990 | 1995 | 2000 | 2005 | 2010 | 2015 | 2020 |

CRISTÓBAL BALENCIAGA

The Spanish fashion visionary revolutionized haute couture with his clean, sculptural lines. His influence is still felt today.

No one characterized the haute couture scene of the forties and fifties as much as Cristóbal Balenciaga. He gave a new silhouette to fashion and was so far ahead of his time that even his colleagues in Paris never spoke of him with anything but complete admiration. "Haute couture is like an orchestra, for which only Balenciaga is the conductor. The rest of us are musicians, following the directions that he gives us." This statement was made by none other than Christian Dior (see page 30).

Cristóbal Balenciaga, the "couturier of couturiers" (another compliment by Christian Dior) was born on January 21, 1895, in the Basque fishing village of Guetaria. His mother, a seamstress, taught him to sew. Encouraged by his first, female fan, the Marquesa de Casa Torres, he began an apprenticeship in couture in Madrid, acquired the Spanish royal family as clients, and at just twenty-four years of age opened his first fashion house in the coastal town of San Sebastián. When the Spanish Civil War broke out in 1936, the designer moved his business to the fashion metropolis of Paris, where Coco Chanel (see page 20) and Elsa Schiaparelli (see page 26) were at the time setting the tone. He moved to number 10 on the fashionable Avenue George V, where the firm's flagship store is still located. From that address he took international high society by storm.

His secret: the finest couture with an eye for perfect proportions. At the beginning of his time in Paris, his style was still very much influenced by his homeland. Torero-style jackets inspired his evening fashions, while gowns such as the famous Infanta dress were reminiscent of the clothing of Spanish princesses in the paintings of Diego Velázquez. But Balenciaga's true greatness became evident when he took leave of the past and looked to the future. The more minimal his designs became, the more groundbreaking they were. When Christian Dior caused a stir with the tiny-waisted hourglass silhouette of his New Look, Cristóbal Balenciaga had already gotten rid of corsets and complicated underskirts. He created the waistless but nevertheless perfectly balanced I-Silhouette, and also the boxy "barrel line." He designed the balloon skirt, jackets with kimono sleeves, the O-shaped cocoon coat, the dart-less sack dress with rounded shoulders, and the baby doll dress. Often his sleeves merged seamlessly into the coat. Long before the word minimalism turned up in the fashion vocabulary of the nineties, he perfected the art of omission in his own unique way. He designed collars so that they stood slightly away from the collarbone, giving the wearer a particularly upright posture. And he dreamed up the seven-eighth-length "bracelet sleeve," allowing the wearer's jewelry to be seen in the best possible light.

The principles of this perfectionist designer, among whose famous assistants were André Courrèges (see page 44), Emanuel Ungaro (see page 56), and Oscar de la Renta (see page 50), were as clear-cut as his designs. He was the most expensive couturier in Paris, he lent out none of his garments, he gave no discounts, and he did not advertise. Nothing and no one was to be allowed to divert attention from his creations—not his studio, which he had furnished in spartan style and whose showroom held only ninety guests, and not even his models. "A dress must be beautiful enough to stand out," he once said, "regardless of the model."

Balenciaga disappeared just as abruptly as he had arrived. When Paris was taken over by mass-produced fashion, the disenchanted couturier, who had always insisted on 100-percent handcrafted work, closed his studio in 1968. He returned to Spain, where he died four years later. His successor, in 1997, was the Frenchman Nicolas Ghesquière, who has today given a new cult status to the house's prêt-à-porter line with a mixture of futurism, drama, austerity, and elegance. But Cristóbal Balenciaga's haute couture remains incomparable to this day.

1895 Born in Guetaria, Spain, on
January 21
1919 Opens a fashion house in
San Sebastián
1937 Opens haute couture house on
Avenue George V in Paris
1947 Creation of the perfume Le Dix
1955 Design of the first tunic dress
1958 Awarded the French Légion
d'Honneur
1968 Designs flight attendants'
uniforms for Air France
1968 Closes his fashion house in Paris
and returns to Spain
1972 Dies in Valencia on March 24

left page
Model Lisa Fonssagrives wears an
evening gown and bolero by Balenciaga

above
Cristóbal Balenciaga, 1927

CHRISTIAN DIOR
DUKE ELLINGTON
KATHARINE HEPBURN

1881 First electric streetcar
in Berlin

1914–18 World War I

1900 Sigmund Freud publishes
The Interpretation of Dreams

1927 Charles Lindbergh crosses
the Atlantic on a non-stop
flight

1867 First issue of *Harper's Bazaar*

| 1855 | 1860 | 1865 | 1870 | 1875 | 1880 | 1885 | 1890 | 1895 | 1900 | 1905 | 1910 | 1915 | 1920 | 1925 | 1930 | 1935 | 1940 |

Typical Dior silhouette: long two-piece
evening gown with mink sleeves

1945 Founding of the United
Nations (UN)

1969 Woodstock music festival in
New York State

1987 Global financial crisis following the
U.S. stock market crash on October 19

1954 Premiere of Alfred Hitchcock's
Rear Window

2003 U.S. invasion of Iraq

1945   1950   1955   1960   1965   1970   1975   1980   1985   1990   1995   2000   2005   2010   2015   2020   2025   2030

CHRISTIAN DIOR

After World War I, the creator of the New Look brought luxury back to wardrobes emptied by war. And, quite incidentally, helped Paris regain its position as the fashion capital.

From a fashion point of view, the fifties had actually began in the forties. To be precise, on February 12, 1947, the date Christian Dior sent out invitations to the presentation of his first collection. As yet, no one suspected that the designer, the son of an industrialist known only to fashion insiders, would unleash nothing less than a sensation.

Dior showed girlishly rounded shoulders, slim waist-lines, and wide, calf-length skirts. His ultra-feminine evening gowns called for up to forty meters of fabric (at a time when in postwar England it was illegal to use more than three meters of fabric for a skirt). For his strikingly modeled silhouettes, he brought back the supposedly long-forgotten lace-up corset. And although—or perhaps precisely because—Dior simply ignored the prevalent style of angular suits with plain short skirts, he touched like no other a nerve of the postwar period conditioned by material shortage. His elegant designs mirrored the longing for a better world of a generation that had only just arisen from the ruins and that a few months earlier had been struggling to survive. Dior at first named his collection simply Ligne Corolle, the Corolla Line, though it went down in history as the New Look, a phrase coined by Carmel Snow, then the editor of the American magazine *Harper's Bazaar*.
But even if Dior turned fashion on its head with his hotly debated debut, his provocative luxury was not revolutionary. Dior created an aesthetic reminiscent of the carefree attitude of the belle époque. The New Look, with a silhouette that seemed impracti-cal for everyday use, took its wearers (and to a degree their emancipation) back into the past. Coco Chanel (see page 20), poster girl for the modern woman of the twentieth century and decided opponent of everything uncomfortable, mocked her contemporary's fashions: "These heavy, stiff dresses that don't even fit into a suitcase—ridiculous! Dior doesn't dress women, he upholsters them."

Dior, however, appeared unimpressed: "Europe has had enough of falling bombs, now it wants to set off fireworks." His aim was to "make elegant women more beautiful and beautiful women more elegant." Seeing himself as a "fighter against mediocrity and the loss of high principles," Dior thought little of austere pragmatism. It was his simple duty "not to give way, to set an example, to be creative in spite of everything." Success proved him right. As early as 1947, Dior had more than a thousand dressmakers working for him, and in 1949 his label accounted for 75 percent of French fashion exports, which repre-sented no less than 5 percent of all French exports. He created twenty-two collections in ten years and changed the silhouette of his clothes each season (the New Look was followed in quick succession by the Tulip and Lily of the Valley lines, and the A-, H-, and Y-line. As early as 1948 he created a

1905 Born in Granville, France,
on January 21
1920–25 Attends Grande École Science
Po in Paris
1928 Opens an art gallery in Paris
showing works by De Chirico,
Braque, and Léger
FROM 1935 Sells designs to Paris
fashion houses and creates
illustrations for the newspaper
Le Figaro
1938–42 Appointed designer at
Robert Piguet
1942–44 Fashion designer at
Lucien Lelong
1947 Shows the first collection under
his own name
1949 Founds Dior New York Inc. and
opens a store in New York
1957 Dies in Montecatini Terme, Italy,
on October 23

left
Cocktail dress with quilted roses

above
Christian Dior in his studio in Paris

pret-à-porter collection for the American market. In addition, he tailored his cuts to the respective physical proportions of his clients in various countries. But Dior, whose career as a couturier did not begin until the age of forty-two (he first studied political science, and worked as a gallery manager and fashion illustrator), did not enjoy his success for long. The master of ladylike elegance died as a result of a heart attack only ten years after his breakthrough. His successors on Avenue Montaigne were, in succession, Yves Saint Laurent (see page 64), Marc Bohan, Gianfranco Ferré, and, finally, John Galliano (see page 132).

Christian Dior with models wearing his clothes, 1950

EMILIO PUCCI

FRED ASTAIRE

ELIZABETH TAYLOR

1874 First Impressionist exhibition in Paris

1890 End of the Indian Wars in the U.S.

1908 The first Ford car, the Model T, comes off the production line in Detroit

1923 Sigmund Freud publishes *The Ego and the Id*

1940 The first McDonald's restaurant opens

| 1865 | 1870 | 1875 | 1880 | 1885 | 1890 | 1895 | 1900 | 1905 | 1910 | 1915 | 1920 | 1925 | 1930 | 1935 | 1940 | 1945 | 1950 |

1954 Premiere of Alfred Hitchcock's
Rear Window

1971 Founding of Greenpeace

1989 The portable game console
Game Boy goes on sale

1997 UN convention on climate change
adopts the Kyoto Protocol

2005 Founding of the Internet
video portal YouTube

1955 1960 1965 1970 1975 1980 1985 1990 1995 2000 2005 2010 2015 2020 2025 2030 2035 2040

EMILIO PUCCI

*With his debonair brand of elegance, in the 1960s the Italian designer became the darling of the international jet set.
His love of patterns made him known as the "Prince of Prints."*

It began with a ski suit—a combination of hooded anorak and a kind of stirrup pants Emilio Pucci had originally designed for himself and which the fashion photographer Toni Frissell liked so much she asked him to design a few more. The images of these ensembles were published in 1948 in the American fashion magazine *Harper's Bazaar*. A few years later, Emilio Pucci developed a new style from the sporty elegance of his first designs: jet-set chic.

The scion of an aristocratic Florentine family with its own palazzo and a family tree going back to Catherine the Great, Pucci had originally aspired to a career in the Italian air force. When in 1950, on account of his unexpected success in the U.S.—the fashion empress Diana Vreeland supported him from the start—he instead opted to become a designer, the Italian aristocracy were up in arms over this unfitting career choice. But there was more to Pucci's meteoric rise from sport-loving pilot officer to visionary fashion designer than his famously convoluted patterns, which had quickly earned him the nickname "Prince of Prints." Other decisive factors were the cuts and fabrics with which he created an entirely new attitude towards life: freedom of movement. Fashion in the fifties was based on the precisely defined model of Parisian haute couture: extremely elegant and perfectly proportioned, yet not particularly practical. As early as 1949, on Capri, he designed a small collection using fabrics modern for the time, such as nylon, which included not only piqué costumes but also swimsuits and cycling shorts. In 1960 Emilio Pucci created lingerie in stretch silk (including the famous "Viva Panty" bodysuit) and close-fitting ski suits in Emilioform, a mixture of shantung silk and nylon he himself invented. He dispensed with underskirts, linings, and padding, and created cuts from geometric forms, leaving it to the flowing fabrics to define the shape of the figure. Tunic dresses of silk jersey, also of his invention, were elegant and easy to wear.

At the same time, of course, they were also extremely light and saved space in the suitcase. Emilio Pucci designed fashions that, decorated with colorful patterns, perfectly suited the optimistic, self-confident attitude toward life in the sixties.
In 1962 he brought out his own couture line, and from then on designed four collections a year. His inspiration, particularly for the intricate patterns he always drew himself, was found in nature, art, and the beauty of distant lands (such as in his African- and Balinese-themed lines). He systematically broke down colors into an infinity of gradations (allegedly more than 500 different ones), giving them names such as Ocean, Moon, Cardinal, and Lavender.

1914 Born in Naples on November 20 as Marchese Emilio Pucci di Barsento
1937 Graduates in political science
1938 Enters the Italian air force
1947 Founding of Emilio Pucci S.r.l. in Florence
1948 Designs a collection of ski clothing published in *Harper's Bazaar*
1949 Presents a swimwear collection
1954 Designs Capri pants, together with loose jerseys and brightly colored, boldly patterned silk scarves
1992 Dies in Florence on November 30

left page
Jersey dress

left
Pucci ensemble with typical design

above
Emilio Pucci

In the mid-seventies, the designer had built up a whole "Pucci world," with carpets, towels, ceramics, and cushion covers. In the eighties, when cool professional dresses set the tone, the rage for vivid patterns began to ebb, but shortly before his death in 1992 his colorful style experienced a revival. Since the start of 2000, the post of top designer at his fashion house has changed repeatedly. In 2008, the Norwegian Peter Dundas was appointed as new creative director. It remains to be seen whether he will succeed in advancing the vision of Emilio Pucci, the inventor of understated elegance, of Capri pants, and of silk jerseys.

left page
Jersey dress and leggings

left
Capri pants

PIERRE BALMAIN

ROBERTO ROSSELLINI

FRANK SINATRA

1898 Spanish-American War

1919 The Treaty of Versailles formally
ends World War I

1880 First issue of the journal *Science*

1909 First seagoing vessel with a diesel engine

1935 Adoption of Nuremberg racial
laws in Nazi German

| 1865 | 1870 | 1875 | 1880 | 1885 | 1890 | 1895 | 1900 | 1905 | 1910 | 1915 | 1920 | 1925 | 1930 | 1935 | 1940 | 1945 | 1950 |

Tweed suit from the fall/winter
collection, 1953

Simone de Beauvoir publishes
The Second Sex

1979 Saddam Hussein becomes
president of Iraq

2008 Kosovo declares independence
from Serbia

1963 Assassination of John F. Kennedy

1995 Massacre at Srebrenica

| 1955 | 1960 | 1965 | 1970 | 1975 | 1980 | 1985 | 1990 | 1995 | 2000 | 2005 | 2010 | 2015 | 2020 | 2025 | 2030 | 2035 | 2040 |

PIERRE BALMAIN

It was thanks to Pierre Balmain that life returned to Parisian haute couture after World War II. In the 1960s his feminine gowns were in high demand among Hollywood stars.

In the fall of 1946 a young French fashion designer left for a lecture tour of the U.S. His mission was to bring buyers and clients back to Paris and make the couture business flourish again. The war years had brought the Paris fashion scene to a near stand-still, and the rich American clientele had turned to designers of their own, such as Main Bocher (see page 24). And so Pierre Balmain saw it as his task to re-conquer the hearts and wallets of the society ladies on the other side of the Atlantic. Of course, he also had something to offer women: a new silhouette.

In 1945, one of his dresses in a completely new cut appeared in American *Vogue*: very feminine, with an ultra-slim waist and a long, lavishly wide, tulle skirt. It was a welcome change after years of skimping on fabric, marked by suits with narrow skirts and square shoulders. The wide, graceful shape of his clothes was exactly what women wanted—exciting-ly different, romantic, and luxurious. Admittedly, in 1947 it was someone else who became famous for this new silhouette, later called the "New Look," his Parisian couturier colleague and friend Christian Dior (see page 30). If one bears in mind that the two legendary designers worked side by side in the same studio for years, it is no surprise that they developed similar ideas and finally, together with Jacques Fath and Cristóbal Balenciaga (see page 28), revived haute couture.

Pierre Balmain, the youngest of the couturiers, had arrived in Paris in the early thirties from Saint-Jean-de-Maurienne in the Savoy Alps. With the original intention of studying architecture, he soon became fascinated with haute couture, which he enthusiasti-cally called the "architecture of movement." He applied to the studio of Edward Molyneux and then moved to Lucien Lelong, with whom Christian Dior had also obtained a position. Both designers dreamed of having their own couture houses and when a chance at funding came along, Pierre

Balmain left Lelong and moved into a studio on Rue François. His first collection, in the fall of 1945, made it straight onto the pages of American *Vogue*. The next step was a branch in New York, where he had prêt-à-porter clothes produced from his couture designs. By 1956 Pierre Balmain had twelve work-shops and approximately 600 employees. His specialty was waisted evening gowns with wide tapering skirts decorated with motifs such as leaves and scrolls. He also introduced another silhouette. Figure-hugging and spreading out only from the knee, it resembled an upturned champagne glass and was his answer to Christian Dior's dome shape.

In 1982, Pierre Balmain, the last of the great fifties couturiers to remain, passed away. Of all the designers who followed him, the Frenchman Christophe Decarnin is probably the most note-worthy. With his razor-sharp rock-star creations, he has been attracting a new generation of celebrities since 2006.

1914 Born in Saint-Jean-de-Maurienne, France, on May 18
1933–34 Studies architecture at the National Academy of Fine Arts in Paris
1934–39 Assistant to Edward Molyneux
1939–45 Together with Christian Dior, responsible for collections at the house of Lucien Lelong
1945 Opens haute couture salon in Paris
1946 Launch of his first perfume, Elysées
1947 Opens an accessories boutique under the name Le Kiosque des Fantaisies
1949 Opens a Balmain store in New York
1977 Sells his business
1982 Dies in Neuilly-sur-Seine on June 29
2006 Christophe Decarnin takes over the creative direction of the house

Pierre Balmain working in his Paris studio, 1965

1876 Alexander Graham Bell invents the telephone

1893–94 Hotel Tassel designed by Viktor Horta built in Brussels

1907–8 Gustav Klimt paints *The Kiss*

1919 The Bauhaus founded in Weimar, Germany

1929 World economic crisis following the U.S. stock market crash on October 25

1939–45 World War II

1870 1875 1880 1885 1890 1895 1900 1905 1910 1915 1920 1925 1930 1935 1940 1945 1950 1955

1965 Forming of the band The Doors

1976 Apple Computer, Inc.
is founded

1990 German reunification

2001 The first "Pop Idol" talent
contest airs on British TV

1960   1965   1970   1975   1980   1985   1990   1995   2000   2005   2010   2015   2020   2025   2030   2035   2040   2045

MISSONI

Rosita and Ottavio Missoni raised the status of knitting to an art form. Their brightly patterned creations became a signature feature of the 1970s.

When Diana Vreeland, the editor of American *Vogue*—a woman who had seen an infinite number of dresses during her career—held her first Missoni dress in her hands in the Grand Hotel in Rome in 1969, she enthusiastically exclaimed, "Look! Who said that only colors exist? There are also tones." She had realized that what she was dealing with here was more than a passing trend. In the hands of Rosita and Ottavio Missoni, knitting, until then considered mainly a domestic, grandmotherly activity, had been transformed into an art form. It was to become the basis for an empire that would one day range from shawls and evening gowns to chairs and even hotels.

The story of Missoni is not only the story of a brand name, but also that of a family. And the two are as closely interwoven as the stitches of their colorful zigzag knitted creations. Significantly, the label was founded in the year in which Ottavio (known as Tai) Missoni and Rosita Jelmini were married—he an Olympic runner with an interest in knitting techniques, she a language student whose family produced shawls and embroidered fabrics. Rosita and Tai met at the 1948 Olympics in London, where he finished sixth in men's hurdles. Back in Italy, their apartment in the small town of Gallarate became their studio. Rosita und Tai experimented with their knitting machines until they were able to produce not only horizontal stripes, but also vertical and diagonal ones, and finally their trademark—zigzag designs. Their Lurex yarns and colorfully zigzagging fashions caused a double dose of excitement at the Missonis' catwalk premiere in Florence in 1967. Their creations, cut with extreme simplicity and at the same time great skill, were a novelty in themselves. But this was nothing next to the sensation caused by their presentation. Rosita had noticed the models' bras showing through the delicate fabrics, and she asked them to wear the designs over their naked skin. While causing a scandal in Florence, at

around the same time in Paris the style was being hailed as one of Yves Saint Laurent's great inventions: the Nude Look (see page 64).

With the support of Italian style icon Anna Piaggi and U.S. fashion queen Diana Vreeland, the Missonis conquered Europe and America. The international press erupted with hymns of praise: "The new status symbol of Italian design" (*New York Times*, 1972), "Museum pieces you can wear" (*Il Giorno*, 1979), "Missoni offers a good reason to come to Milan" (*Women's Wear Daily*, 1974). In the process, the Missonis gave the seventies two important stylistic landmarks: an uncomplicated glamour emerging from the combination of intricate patterns and easy-to-wear designs (knitwear stretches and requires no darts), and the concept of mix and match. When Rosita and Tai decided in 1974 that from then on they would hold their shows only in Milan, near their company headquarters, the international fashion business followed. Rome and Florence had been superseded as fashion capitals.

In designing their Paris boutique, it was discovered that Missoni's elaborate fabrics also seemed ideal for living in: tapestries, upholstery textiles, cushions—the colorful stripes, waves, zigzags, and flames produced a sensational overall effect. The Home Collection, created in 1981, was the pride and joy of Rosita Missoni, who handed over her role as designer of the fashion lines to her daughter Angela in 1998. Angela's brothers Vittorio and Luca also work for the business, and Angela's eldest daughter Margherita, her mother's muse, is known as an ambassador for the brand, drawing attention to the beauty of the skillful designs. It all began with twelve colors per collection; there are now as many as forty. Who knows what the third generation of Missonis will knit.

1921 Ottavio Missoni born in Ragusa, Italy, on February 11
1931 Rosita Jelmini, later Missoni, born in Golasecca, Italy, on November 20
1948 Rosita and Ottavio meet at the London Olympics
1953 Marriage of Rosita and Ottavio and opening of a small knitting workshop
1958 First collection sold to the department store La Rinascente in Milan
1979 Presents first men's collection
1980 Introduction of lines of home textiles, wall hangings, and decorative and furnishing fabrics
1998 Daughter Angela takes over as creative director

left page
Knitted beach outfit in zigzag design

above
Rosita and Ottavio Missoni

left
Missoni campaign, 2002

right page
Kate Moss in typical Missoni knitwear

1903 Founding of the Kraft Foods
company

1928–30 Construction of the Chrysler Building in
New York, designed by William van Alen

1957 Ghana becom
the first Afri
colony to ac
independenc
after World V

1882 First electric streetlights
in Berlin

1917 October Revolution in Russia

1942 Edward Hopper
paints *Nighthawks*

| 1875 | 1880 | 1885 | 1890 | 1895 | 1900 | 1905 | 1910 | 1915 | 1920 | 1925 | 1930 | 1935 | 1940 | 1945 | 1950 | 1955 | 1960 |

Dress in graphic style, Milan, 1968

1966–76 Chinese Cultural Revolution

1979 NATO Double-Track Decision

1995 The first fully computer-animated film, *Toy Story*, shown in cinemas

2004 George W. Bush re-elected U.S. president

| 1965 | 1970 | 1975 | 1980 | 1985 | 1990 | 1995 | 2000 | 2005 | 2010 | 2015 | 2020 | 2025 | 2030 | 2035 | 2040 | 2045 | 2050 |

ANDRÉ COURRÈGES

This designer created clothing with purist vigor in austere geometric forms. His futuristic "Space Fashion" encapsulated the 1960s' euphoric mood.

In January 1965 André Courrèges presented a collection that was to catapult fashion into the future at the speed of light. It was a collection that looked as though it had come straight from the moon. Pin-sharp lines, geometric cuts, no ornamentation to speak of, and a brilliant white. Dresses, skirts, and coats in an austere A-line were combined with white goggles, hats, and plain, thigh-high patent leather boots. But that was not all. Something else emerged from this "space age collection" to make its first official appearance on a French catwalk: the knee. André Courrèges raised skirt hems so high they became miniskirts.

This man seemingly from the future actually came from the town of Pau in the south of France. Courrèges discovered his fascination with fashion, in particular the fashion of Balenciaga, when he moved to Paris as a freshly qualified civil engineer at the age of twenty-two. There he discovered the Spanish designer Cristóbal Balenciaga (see page 28). For eleven years he worked in the couturier's strict school of style, where he not only mastered the art of tailoring but also met his future wife and business partner, Coqueline Barrière. In 1961 he left the famous studio on Avenue George V to found his own couture house with her. Soon the Frenchman had stripped off his teacher's corseted style and put his own fashion vision into practice: modern clothing for the modern, active woman. First he designed form-fitting women's pants cut in a casual masculine style for both daytime and nighttime. Then came the miniskirt, celebrated at the same time in London as Mary Quant's invention (see page 58). The knitted all-in-one body stocking followed.

What must have seemed at the time like a succession of provocations (after all, severely tailored full skirts with stiffened underskirts were still worn in the 1950s) was a highly calculated move. André Courrèges, the engineer who constructed rather than tailored his fashions, had worked out what the woman of the sixties needed: freedom of movement. This he gave her, by creating styles with room to maneuver. His short A-line dresses and coats—often of thick gabardine and later of modern materials such as vinyl—needed no darts and were not restricting. His new skirt lengths and flats liberated the legs, as did the all-in-one body stocking. The only decoration allowed by the purist Courrèges, apart from occasional daisies, stripes, and checks, were machine-stitched seams revealing the garments' construction.

In 1965 André Courrèges decided to close his house for two years both to the press and to buyers. His first collection created so much attention that his designs had been frequently copied. In 1967 he was back with "Couture Future," a modern, mass-produced prêt-à-porter line—another forward-looking idea. But in terms of fashion, the designer was not progressing. In 1986 he had to close down his couture line. He staged several comebacks, including one in the early nineties, but today the label maintains a low profile. Nevertheless, his style is still highly influential in today's fashion world. André Courrèges' visionary quality can quite clearly be seen in this quotation: "At first, people were shocked by the airplane, now everyone takes them. Women don't wear pants to the office yet, but they will." It dates from 1964.

1923 Born in Pau, France, on March 9
BEFORE 1945 Studies civil engineering
1950–61 Apprenticeship in couture and assistant to Cristóbal Balenciaga in Paris
1962 Opens a salon in Paris
1967 Launches three lines: "Prototype" (made-to-measure), "Couture Future" (luxury ready-to-wear), "Hyperbole" (ready-to-wear)
1971 Launch of first perfume, Empreintes
1972 Designs clothing for French participants in the Munich Olympics
1973 Presents his first men's collection
1974 Opens a store in New York
1985 His business is acquired by the Japanese group Itokin
1994 Jean-Charles de Castelbajac takes over as creative director

André Courrèges, 1968

GRETA GARBO

AUDREY HEPBURN

1885 Mark Twain publishes *The Adventures of Huckleberry Finn*

1918 U.S. president Wilson presents his Fourteen Points program

1948 Berlin Airlift

1901 First Nobel Prize awarded by the King of Sweden in Stockholm

1930 Mahatma Gandhi leads the Salt March in protest against the British salt monopoly

1953 First successful ascent of Mount Everest

| 1875 | 1880 | 1885 | 1890 | 1895 | 1900 | 1905 | 1910 | 1915 | 1920 | 1925 | 1930 | 1935 | 1940 | 1945 | 1950 | 1955 | 1960 |

Audrey Hepburn as Holly Golightly in the famous little black dress, 1961

1969 Stonewall uprising on Christopher
Street in New York

1995 Oslo Peace Accords between
Israel and the PLO

1980–88 Iran-Iraq War

2005 Death of Pope John Paul II and election of his
successor Joseph Ratzinger as Pope Benedict XVI

1965 | 1970 | 1975 | 1980 | 1985 | 1990 | 1995 | 2000 | 2005 | 2010 | 2015 | 2020 | 2025 | 2030 | 2035 | 2040 | 2045 | 2050

HUBERT DE GIVENCHY

Every artist has his muse: Audrey Hepburn made Hubert de Givenchy's elegantly simple creations world famous.

What makes a dress a complete success? If you ask the fashion designer Hubert de Givenchy, it is first of all the fabric, handled with the utmost care. Without understanding a material's particular nature, even the most imaginative design would be doomed to fail. And indeed, bringing a fabric to life, shaping it with respect and elegance, is the secret behind the perfection of Givenchy's designs.

If his father had had his way, the later master couturier would probably never have designed a single dress. Monsieur Givenchy senior, a government employee, wanted his son to become a lawyer. But luckily, Givenchy was inspired by the elegance of his fashion-conscious mother, studied fashion design at the École des Beaux Arts in Paris, and worked with Jacques Fath, Robert Piguet, and Elsa Schiaparelli (see page 26). At barely twenty-four years of age he opened his own salon on the Plaine Monceau in Paris. Financially self-reliant from the beginning, Givenchy found the costly couture fabrics for which he would become famous well outside his budget. Lacking funds, he designed his first collection in simple linen, raffia, cotton, and woven straw. And he remained faithful to his principle of working only with and never against the material. The result was his trademark: unpretentious elegance, perfectly executed.

Givenchy was respected from the outset for his skill, but worldwide fame found him with Audrey Hepburn, whom he met in 1953 on the set of the film *Sabrina*. Even though he was soon afterwards to design for greats such as Jacqueline Kennedy (whose legendary ensemble at John F. Kennedy's funeral was by Givenchy) and Grace Kelly, it was the fine-boned Hepburn who became his muse. Fascinated by her natural grace and unassuming charm, he created a style that underlined her natural beauty with simple, straight lines and high waistlines. Hepburn repaid him with lifelong loyalty: both privately and in her films, the actress exclusively wore the creations of her Parisian house couturier.

In 1996, eight years after he sold his house to the French luxury goods group LVMH, Hubert de Givenchy bade a final farewell to the world of fashion. In 2006 he put up for auction what was probably his most famous creation: that little black dress in which Audrey Hepburn looked so ravishing in the opening scene of the film classic *Breakfast at Tiffany's*. This forty-two-year-old, unadorned sheath dress in heavy Italian satin sold for $807,000 at Christie's auction house in London to an unknown bidder, making it to date the most expensive dress in the world.

1927 Born in Beauvais, France,
on February 21
1945–51 Assistant to Jacques Fath,
Robert Piguet, Elsa Schiaparelli
1952 Opens haute couture studio
in Paris and presents his first
collection
FROM 1954 Personal stylist to the
actress Audrey Hepburn
1955 Launch of his first perfume,
L'Interdit
FROM 1968 Introduction of prêt-à-
porter collections
1988 Business acquired by the LVMH
group
1995 Retires from the fashion business

Hubert de Givenchy, mid-1980s

1906 Henri Matisse paints
Le bonheur de vivre

1920–30 Harlem Renaissance

1938 Discovery of atomic fission by
Otto Hahn and Fritz Strassmann

1894–95 First Sino-Japanese War

1932 Founding of the Kingdom
of Saudi Arabia

1949 Premiere of Arthur Miller's play
Death of a Salesman

| 1880 | 1885 | 1890 | 1895 | 1900 | 1905 | 1910 | 1915 | 1920 | 1925 | 1930 | 1935 | 1940 | 1945 | 1950 | 1955 | 1960 | 1965 |

Beverly Johnson presents a long pastel
dress by Roy Halston, January 1975

966–73 Construction of the World
Trace Center in New York

1977 Opening of Studio 54
in New York

1995 Sweden, Finland, and Austria
join the European Union

2001 First same-sex marriage in
the Netherlands

1970 1975 1980 1985 1990 1995 2000 2005 2010 2015 2020 2025 2030 2035 2040 2045 2050 2055

ROY HALSTON

In the 1970s he made American fashion world famous with his luxurious yet simple creations.

A slender evening gown in cashmere. Unsurpassed in simplicity, comfort, and luxuriousness. Some may think this sounds boring. In the late sixties, when frilly hippie clothing set the tone, it was revolutionary. Roy Halston's minimalist creations took America by storm. Stars from Hollywood to Broadway followed in his wake, bringing the uncomplicated, sporty glamour of his clothes to the world. "Fashion starts with fashionable people," Halston once said. Always in the limelight, with a following that included Lauren Bacall, Bianca Jagger, Liza Minnelli, and Elizabeth Taylor, he can be rightly described as the U.S.'s first star designer. But also as the one who lifted typical, casual American chic to a whole new level: to the heights of haute couture.

Roy Halston Frowick, born in 1932 in Des Moines, Iowa, was originally a milliner. After breaking off his studies at the Art Institute of Chicago, he opened a hat shop in the fifties. In 1957 he moved to New York and after a short time ended up in the milliner studio of the famous department store Bergdorf Goodman. For nine years Halston was responsible for 150 hat-makers and designed famous head coverings like the pillbox hat Jackie Kennedy wore at her husband's presidential inauguration.

At Bergdorf Goodman Halston not only came to know the stars he skillfully deployed as high-profile marketing tools for the unostentatious clothes of his meteoric but short-lived career as a designer, but he also experienced first-hand what women wanted. Not any women, but American women. By comparison with their European counterparts, they were ahead of their time, more independent and self-confident. Halston realized that these "power ladies" did not need complicated creations in the Parisian couture style, but a look that suited their active lifestyle. In 1966 he launched his first fashion collection for the luxury department store. Two years later he parted from his employer and started his own women's line, which included ready-made as well as made-to-measure items, and was an instant hit.

Apart from the casual cashmere dresses, slender pantsuits, and floor-length jersey garments that naturally enveloped the body, he had one of his greatest successes with shirt dresses made in the newly developed Ultrasuede, a fine, washable imitation suede fabric. Although his creations appeared simple, they were full of hidden subtleties. Bias cutting and an infallible instinct for emphasizing women's feminine assets (and masking their weaknesses) were the strengths of this American couturier.

In the mid-seventies the designer was a star as famous as his clients. The turning point came with the opening of Studio 54. Halston became caught up in a whirl of parties and drugs—and in a deal for a low-priced store collection. The luxury fashion world of the early eighties had no understanding for cheap secondary lines. In 1983 Halston was forced to give up his job as creative director of his company, and seven years later he died at the age of only fifty-seven. Most attempts to breathe new life into the legendary label have so far petered out.

1932 Born in Des Moines, Iowa, on
April 23
FROM 1952 Studies at the Art Institute
in Chicago
1957 Opens his first store in Chicago
and moves to New York
1957–58 Assistant to the milliner
Lilly Daché in New York
1958–66 Makes hats for upscale NY
department store Bergdorf
Goodman
1966–68 Complete Halston fashion line
for Bergdorf Goodman
1968 Founds his own business
1982 Designs a low-budget collection
for the U.S. department store
chain J. C. Penney
1990 Dies in New York on March 26

Roy Halston (born Roy Halston Frowick),
1978

OSCAR DE LA RENTA

FEDERICO FELLINI

PAUL MCCARTNEY

1909 Sergei Diaghilev founds the
Ballets Russes in Paris

1939 Margaret Mitchell's *Gone with the Wind*
filmed by David O. Selznick

1892 First issue of American *Vogue*

1923 Founding of the USSR

1954 First commercial atomic po
station begins operations
Obninsk near Moscow

| 1880 | 1885 | 1890 | 1895 | 1900 | 1905 | 1910 | 1915 | 1920 | 1925 | 1930 | 1935 | 1940 | 1945 | 1950 | 1955 | 1960 | 1965 |

Azure blue gown from the fall
collection in New York Fashion
Week, 2007

1993 Bill Clinton becomes 42nd U.S. president

1968 Assassination of Martin Luther King

2007–9 Global financial crisis

1983 Discovery of the HIV virus

2000 The dot-com bubble bursts

1970 1975 1980 1985 1990 1995 2000 2005 2010 2015 2020 2025 2030 2035 2040 2045 2050 2055

OSCAR DE LA RENTA

He was the first American designer to create haute couture for a Paris fashion house. For decades his glamorous dresses have embodied Upper East Side chic, the style of New York's high society.

At the age of eighteen he was already dressing "like a gentleman"—custom-made suit, necktie, gold tiepin, the works. Nothing has changed. Since 1965 Oscar de la Renta has been designing glamorous gowns for American high society and has dressed four First Ladies (Jackie Kennedy, Nancy Reagan, Hillary Clinton, and Laura Bush). He is the president and creative director of a fashion business that despite the economic crisis had sales of 100 million dollars in 2008. The story of Oscar de la Renta is one hundred percent American Dream. It is the story of a Latino boy who grew up with six sisters in the Dominican Republic, moved to Madrid at the age of eighteen to study painting, became an assistant to Balenciaga (see page 28), and ten years later plunged into the world of Paris haute couture at the side of Lanvin designer Antonio Castillo—and who, finally, founded his own label in New York at the age of thirty-three.

Today his company headquarters in Manhattan's Garment District shares a building with two other American design stars, Ralph Lauren (see page 74) and Donna Karan (see page 104). It was not only talent but also his business sense that could be seen early on. Oscar de la Renta left the fashion metropolis of Paris after only three years with the firm resolve to transplant his knowledge of haute couture to New York, the city of endless possibilities, in the form of a ready-to-wear line of his own. He had understood that haute couture is the icing on the cake of fashion, but prêt-à-porter is the cake itself. Diana Vreeland, then editor in chief of American *Vogue*, was able to convince him that he should spend a few more years training as designer of Elizabeth Arden's custom-tailored line. In 1965 he at last founded his own fashion house. Five years later, one couldn't have imagined the New York fashion scene without him.

His style is still reminiscent of the Paris school. Oscar de la Renta is known for precise, figure-flattering tailoring, and for extravagant details such as ruffles and appliqué. Combined with his Latin American preference for strong colors and his typically American instinct for wearability, this is the secret of his enduring success over several decades. And it is also the reason why in 1993 Balmain (see page 38) knocked on his door. He became the first American designer to create haute couture for a Paris fashion house. His own business has also benefited from the experience. For him quality is just as important as efficiency. Instead of employing fourteen seamstresses with two sewing machines as at Balmain (where almost everything was hand-made), in his New York studio he gave each seamstress her own sewing machine so, he said, "We can make those dreamy fantasies a reality for many more women."

Unlike many of his designer colleagues, Oscar de la Renta has so far not put himself in the hands of a major corporation. He relies on the power of the family. His son-in-law Alex Bolen is his chief executive, his stepdaughter Eliza Bolen as creative director is responsible for licensing, and his adopted son Moises works in the design studio. This guarantees the future of Oscar de la Renta's philosophy: "I have always felt my role as a designer is to do the very best I can for a woman to make her look her best. Fashion is only fashion once a woman puts it on."

1932 Born in Santo Domingo on July 22
FROM 1950 Begins studying painting in Madrid and learns fashion design under Cristóbal Balenciaga
1960–63 Assistant to the fashion designer Antonio Castillo at Lanvin in Paris
1963 Moves to New York and works for Elizabeth Arden, Christian Dior, and Diana Vreeland
1965 Founding of Oscar de la Renta Ltd. in New York
1977 Creation of his first perfume, Oscar
1993–2002 Artistic director of the Paris fashion house Pierre Balmain
SINCE 2001 Introduction of several Oscar de la Renta lines for accessories, furniture, domestic textiles, and bridal fashions

Oscar de la Renta, 2001

1889 Vincent van Gogh paints *Starry Night*

1921 F. W. Murnau's film *Nosferatu* creates the vampire film genre

1948 The U.S. Congress adopts the Marshall Plan

1904–5 Russo-Japanese War

1936–39 Spanish Civil War

| 1880 | 1885 | 1890 | 1895 | 1900 | 1905 | 1910 | 1915 | 1920 | 1925 | 1930 | 1935 | 1940 | 1945 | 1950 | 1955 | 1960 | 1965 |

Sasha Pivovarova wearing a piece from the fall/winter 2007 collection by Valentino

960 17 African colonies win independence
from their colonial powers

1983 Civil War begins in Sudan

1998 Founding of the online file-sharing site Napster

1974 Steven Spielberg's career takes
off with the film *Jaws*

2007 Romania and Bulgaria become the 26th and
27th member states of the European Union

1970   1975   1980   1985   1990   1995   2000   2005   2010   2015   2020   2025   2030   2035   2040   2045   2050   2055

VALENTINO GARAVANI

"Rosso Valentino" is the only color to have been named after a fashion designer. The Italian-born Valentino Garavani is famous for trend-resistant, dramatic gowns that envelop the wearer in sumptuous luxury.

He was the last of his kind—a designer who learned his craft from the bottom up, and, together with Christian Dior (see page 30), Coco Chanel (see page 20), and Yves Saint Laurent (see page 64), shaped the world of haute couture. One who, quite naturally, continued to hold on to his place on the fast-moving fashion scene even when a new generation of designers had moved into the place of the previous one. And who finally, after almost fifty years of successful devotion to fashion, announced that he "preferred to leave parties when people are still dancing." With these words he presented his last collection in Paris in September 2007 at the age of seventy-five. Valentino Garavani, better known by only his first name, decided to bid an elegant farewell at the height of his career, rather than await the decline that by his own account was inevitable. Typical Valentino. The North Italian-born designer with the carefully blow-dried hair is not someone to leave his life decisions to be made by others. Neither does he take any notice of those around him when it is a question of one thing: his style.

His work, according to Garavani, is comparable to that of a writer. Except that over the years he has been writing only one story, that of his style. And the collections? They are to be understood as individual chapters of the story, with all their impressions, ideas, and motifs. This couturier, who began his career as a simple fashion illustrator and, after working with Jean Dessès and Guy Laroche, led his fashion empire from Rome together with his partner in business and life, Giancarlo Giammetti, seems to be resistant to trends. Trends, in his view, are "only something for very young people and for those who are perhaps a sort of fashion victim." He himself would try "to create a young creation—glamorous, sexy, extremely feminine— not clothes that last only for a short, short season."

It sometimes seems Garavani would have preferred time had stood still—in an era when women still lived for glamour and it was unthinkable for stars to present themselves in the casual look favored by today's public, when Jacqueline Kennedy wore one of his creations to marry the Greek billionaire Aristotle Onassis, and the *dolce vita* reigned in Rome. Valentino's gowns always look as though their wearers were about to receive an Oscar (something that has indeed happened on several occasions).

His creations are elegant and dignified, always luxuriously cut, often embroidered with beads or sequins, or worked in lace. The couturier prefers intense colors: white, black, red (the "Rosso Valentino" Italian *Vogue* said was impossible to find on any color chart).

Whether a suitable successor can be found to head the fashion house is not clear. The young Italian Alessandra Facchinetti (formerly at Gucci) was unable to make her mark. It remains to be seen whether Maria Grazia Chiuri and Pier Paolo Piccioli can fill Valentino's shoes. The master himself, meanwhile, has been far from idle since his retirement from the world of fashion: his luxurious lifestyle (he is considered a legendary host) is almost as famous as his gowns.

1932 Born in Voghera, Italy, on May 11
as Valentino Clemente Ludovico
Garavani
1950 Studies at the École de la
Chambre Syndicale de la Couture
Parisienne
1951–56 Assistant to Jean Dessès
and Guy Laroche in Paris
1959 Returns to Italy and opens
haute couture salon in Rome
1962 First fashion show in Palazzo Pitti
in Florence
1968 Creates wedding dress for
Jacqueline Kennedy for her
marriage to Aristotle Onassis
1970 Introduces a prêt-à-porter line
1972 Introduces a men's line and a
range of decorative textiles
1978 Launch of the first perfume,
Valentino
1998 Sells his business
2007 Hands over artistic direction
of the fashion house

Valentino Garavani, 2009

Back view of a gown in "Rosso
Valentino" from the spring/summer
2004 haute couture collection

1891 Opening of Carnegie Hall
in New York

1903 First Tour de France

1917 U.S. enters World War I

1925 F. Scott Fitzgerald publishes
The Great Gatsby

1938 The *Hindenburg*, the largest flying machine ever built,
crashes during approach at Lakehurst, New Jersey

1955 Arrest of Rosa Parks tri
the Montgomery Bus Be

1880 1885 1890 1895 1900 1905 1910 1915 1920 1925 1930 1935 1940 1945 1950 1955 1960 1965

Emanuel Ungaro campaign

1987–93 First Intifada in Palestine

1967 Racial unrest in many U.S. cities

1979 Margaret Thatcher becomes prime minister of the United Kingdom

2002 U.S. detention camp set up at Guantánamo

| 1970 | 1975 | 1980 | 1985 | 1990 | 1995 | 2000 | 2005 | 2010 | 2015 | 2020 | 2025 | 2030 | 2035 | 2040 | 2045 | 2050 | 2055 |

EMANUEL UNGARO

In the 1960s, Ungaro's carefree mix of patterns and feminine draped dresses brought gaiety back to the austere Paris couture scene.

"Someone must find a way to make modern, contemporary clothes or we shall end up boring people to death," said Emanuel Ungaro just before the opening of his 1973 fashion show. For nearly another thirty years he was to ensure that imagination, sensuality, and the principle of "more is more" stirred up the fashion world. His artfully draped dresses clinging to womanly curves, his opulent cocktail gowns, his love of bold colors and wild pattern mixes, ensured that his designs—sometimes very tough, sometimes very romantic—always made a statement.

In the early sixties, Cristóbal Balenciaga (see page 28) ruled Parisian haute couture with his visionary designs and unshakeable rigor. In a monastic atmosphere, he and his assistants invariably produced two collections a year. Among the Balenciaga disciples in their white coats was an ambitious young man from Aix-en-Provence who learned to sew from his father, a custom tailor, and had taken his master craftsman's diploma at the tender age of twenty-two: Emanuel Ungaro.

It is astonishing that a designer who reveled in colors and shapes had emerged from such a disciplined school of style. In 1965, after six years with Balenciaga and a short period of employment with André Courrèges (see page 44), Ungaro, the son of Italian parents, set himself up in his own couture studio, with little money and four seamstresses. Two influential factors favored his start: there was great international interest in the trends from the French metropolis, and Italian textile manufacturers supported him with the hopes of gaining a foothold in Paris fashion. It worked. After only two years, Ungaro moved with his studio onto elegant Avenue Montaigne, still the headquarters of his business, opened a boutique, and in 1968 launched his first prêt-à-porter collection.

Initially still under the influence of the highly stylized aesthetic of Balenciaga and Courrèges, during the hippie era Emanuel Ungaro soon found his personal style. With carefree pattern mixes, transparent blouses, and colorful circle skirts, he brought provocation and good humor to the catwalk of the seventies. He easily made the leap from the flower child to the power woman, setting the tone in the eighties with black and white dotted fabrics and overly accentuated shoulders.

In 2001, the designer abandoned prêt-à-porter and handed over his seven men's and women's fashion lines to younger hands. Since then, the position of lead designer at his fashion house has been a revolving door. In 2004, the haute couture collection was finally discontinued. Emanuel Ungaro justified this decision, which also meant his retirement, by saying that it no longer had anything to do with the realities of the fashion market.

1933 Born in Aix-en-Provence, France, on February 13
1955 Moves to Paris
1958–61 Assistant to Cristóbal Balenciaga
1961–62 Assistant to André Courrèges
1965 Opens haute couture salon in Paris
1969 Introduces a prêt-à-porter line
1973 Introduces his first men's collection
1983 Launch of his first perfume, Diva
1996 Sells label to the Salvatore Ferragamo company, continuing as artistic director
2001 Retires from prêt-à-porter
2004 Closes down the haute couture line

Emanuel Ungaro in his studio, 2002

1902 Alfred Stieglitz founds the
Photo-Secession in New York

1930–31 Construction of the Empire State Building
in New York, designed by William van Alen

1954 J. R. R. Tolkien publishes
The Lord of the Rings

1895 Wilhelm Conrad Roentgen
discovers X-rays

1921 Albert Einstein receives
the Nobel Prize for Physics

1943 First New York Fashion Week

1880 1885 1890 1895 1900 1905 1910 1915 1920 1925 1930 1935 1940 1945 1950 1955 1960 1965

1979 Islamic Revolution in Iran under the
leadership of the Ayatollah Khomeini

1968 Violent suppression of the Prague
Spring in Czechoslovakia

1990–91 Persian Gulf War

SINCE 2007 The Burj Dubai in Dubai is the tallest
building in the world at 2,684 feet

1970   1975   1980   1985   1990   1995   2000   2005   2010   2015   2020   2025   2030   2035   2040   2045   2050   2055

MARY QUANT

This British designer is considered the inventor of the miniskirt. Her designs are emblematic of the lifestyle of the Swinging Sixties.

Whether in Paris, New York, or Milan, these days the clothes shown during Fashion Week usually have one thing in common: the models on the catwalk are all quite naked. Low-backed gowns slide down to expose the derrière, tops reveal more than they cover, and dresses are often so short they could be mistaken for little tops. The most striking thing about these creations, however, is the reaction they provoke—no one today seems to be bothered. In this "generation of indifference" one could almost wish oneself back to the middle of the last century, when only an inch or so of missing fabric could set off a revolution.

It all began in 1955, when the art student Mary Quant, together with her later husband, the aristocrat Alexander Plunket Greene, and their business partner, Archie McNair, opened the Bazaar fashion boutique on King's Road in London's Chelsea district. Quant, then twenty-one years old, the daughter of a teacher, had planned to sell ready-made clothing from wholesalers, which she would alter to her own style. But when she found that everything she had bought in the morning and altered in the afternoon had completely sold out by evening, she began to produce her own clothing. She transformed her small apartment into a studio (it was not until 1963 that she began to manufacture on a large scale), where her Siamese cat gnawed on the patterns produced of a paper made of fish derivatives. What survived became the foundation for global success: the skirts that each year grew increasingly shorter. Quant created a "total look" that emphasized the legs (preferably slim) rather than classic feminine curves. Her waistless, child-like, loose-fitting dresses and schoolgirl tunics were characterized by clean lines and high armholes. The new dress lengths were worn with flat buckled shoes or boots—Quant considered high heels to be instruments of torture. The revolutionary, abbreviated hemlines quickly became the symbol

of the Swinging Sixties, of rebellion against the establishment (which dutifully reacted with a storm of indignation), and women's liberation.

Quant was celebrated (or demonized, according to one's point of view) as the inventor of the miniskirt, although with Marc Bohan and André Courrèges (see page 44) hems had also been rising in Paris. But Mary Quant had a few advantages over the French couturiers: she was young, innovative, and above all in the right place at the right time—London, the "coolest" city in the world at the time, where the true originators of the miniskirt incidentally lived—the girls of the street.

In the late sixties the miniskirt shrank even further to a micro-mini, but by that time the commotion had long subsided. In California, the first flower children were already being seen in their long, flowing skirts. Quant's reaction was to close her London boutiques and concentrate on developing her makeup line. When she was asked recently what she preferred to wear, she replied: "Trousers, T-shirts, and jackets."

1934 Born in Blackheath, England, on February 11
BEFORE 1955 Studies illustration at Goldsmith's College in London
1955 Opens the boutique Bazaar on London's King's Road with her later husband Alexander Plunket Greene
1959 Opens a second boutique in Knightsbridge in London
1966 Introduces a cosmetics line
1969 Discontinues her fashion line and continues to run her business with accessory, lingerie, and cosmetic lines
1970 introduces interior and textile design collections
1974 Launch of her first perfume, Havoc
2000 Sells her business

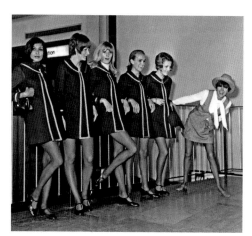

left page
Fall collection, London, 1971

left
Mary Quant with models at Heathrow Airport, shortly before her international fashion tour, 1968

above
Mary Quant, 1966

1903 The Wright brothers, Wilbur and Orville,
make the first engine-powered flight

1933 The National Socialists take
power in Germany

1959 The first Barbie
doll is presented
at the New York
toy fair

1892 The Coca-Cola Company
is founded

1946 First International Film
Festival in Cannes

1919–33 Prohibition in the U.S.

| 1880 | 1885 | 1890 | 1895 | 1900 | 1905 | 1910 | 1915 | 1920 | 1925 | 1930 | 1935 | 1940 | 1945 | 1950 | 1955 | 1960 | 1965 |

On the red carpet: Hilary Swank in an steel-grey
Armani gown

1973 First commercial personal
computer

1996 First cloned mammal (Dolly the sheep)

1990 End of the Cold War declared by
34 nations of the Conference on
Security and Co-operation in Europe

2009 Barack Obama becomes the first
African-American president of the U.S.

| 1970 | 1975 | 1980 | 1985 | 1990 | 1995 | 2000 | 2005 | 2010 | 2015 | 2020 | 2025 | 2030 | 2035 | 2040 | 2045 | 2050 | 2055 |

GIORGIO ARMANI

The Italian designer symbolizes reduced forms and neutral colors. He is seen as paving the way for modern, minimalistic design.

His name is as much part of Hollywood as the stars on the legendary Walk of Fame. There is no Oscar ceremony without at least one of his glamorous evening gowns sparkling in the sea of popping flash-bulbs, hardly an Armani fashion show without at least one world-famous film star sitting in the front row. Since the late eighties when Michelle Pfeiffer and Jodie Foster were the first to appear in his creations at the Academy Awards, the red carpet and the permanently tan Giorgio Armani have been inseparable. The designer is known as a living legend, as a master of non-colors and the inventor of casual elegance.

The cinema has always played an important role in the designer's life, not only as a springboard for his career, but also as a stylistic model and inspiration. As a child, the fashion icon, who grew up in humble circumstances in Piacenza, northern Italy, made regular trips to nearby Milan to see screen classics by Alfred Hitchcock and Luchino Visconti. There, for the first time, he encountered the world that was one day to become his home: Hollywood. He is still passionate about old films, and his collections often reflect the glamour of the forties and fifties. What is today an unparalleled success story was, in reality, not even remotely planned. After abandoning his medical studies in 1957, Armani worked as a window dresser and buyer at the Milan department store La Rinascente. He learned to think in economic terms and recognize the tastes of clients, lessons from which he would later profit as a designer. When he made the acquaintance of Nino Cerruti, he switched sides—from fashion buyer to fashion designer. Without any formal training in tailoring, he designed the men's line for the Italian clothing enterprise. In 1975, together with his life partner, Sergio Galeotti, who was also his business partner, he founded the firm of Giorgio Armani S.p.A. He presented his first collection in 1975 with a focus on elegant suits in muted colors,

which perfectly suited the casually elegant mood of the time.

In the eighties, when the professional and athletic looks moved into the social foreground, Giorgio Armani was one of the first on the scene. He removed the stiff linings from suit jackets, gave them a loose fit, and replaced the shirt and tie with a simple t-shirt. He also revolutionized women's fashions, delivering exactly what the newly liberated woman needed: a "power suit" that did not look like a man's suit. With his preference for neutral colors and clean lines, he cleared the way for other minimalist designers such as Calvin Klein (see page 86) and Jil Sander (see page 94). His international breakthrough finally came in 1980 with his costumes for the film *American Gigolo*.

Giorgio Armani's empire now encompasses eight fashion lines, the haute couture line Giorgio Armani Privé, the home collection Armani Casa, countless fragrances, cosmetic products, illustrated books, watches, and even chocolates. There are Armani hotels, bars, and spas, mobile phones, and even cars designed by Armani. Since the death of Sergio Galeotti in 1985, Giorgio Armani stands alone at the head of an enterprise with more than 5,000 staff members and some 500 stores worldwide. The firm's headquarters is a 12,000-square-meter Renaissance palazzo in Milan, the so-called Fortezza Armani. Even if Giorgio Armani's business is wide-ranging, he maintains his concept of restrained elegance in his private life. He is rarely seen in jet-setting circles or at fashion parties. And in contrast to his gowns, so far he has only twice attended an Oscar ceremony. "My stars," he once said in an interview, "are the dresses."

1934 Born in Piacenza, Italy, on July 11
1957 Window dresser and soon afterward fashion buyer for the Milan department store La Rinascente
1961–70 Assistant at Nino Cerruti
1975 Founding of Giorgio Armani S.p.A. with Sergio Galeotti in Milan
1980 Costume designer for Richard Gere in the film *American Gigolo*
1982 Launch of his first perfume, Armani
1985 After the death of Sergio Galeotti, Armani takes over his share in the business
2005 Founding of Armani Hotels & Resorts

Giorgio Armani

left
Giorgio Armani fall/winter
2009/10 collection

right page
Giorgio Armani spring/summer
2010 collection

1911 Roald Amundsen becomes
first to reach the geographic
South Pole

1895 First Venice Biennale

1932 Aldous Huxley publishes
Brave New World

1956 Brigitte Bardot makes h
international breakthro
with *And God Created Wo*

1923 First issue of *Time* magazine

1948 Declaration of Human Rights by
the UN General Assembly

1880 1885 1890 1895 1900 1905 1910 1915 1920 1925 1930 1935 1940 1945 1950 1955 1960 1965

1973 First oil crisis   1999 War in Kosovo

1982 Production of the first   2006 In Liberia, Ellen Johnson-Sirleaf is sworn
      commercial CD player   in as the first female African head of state

1970   1975   1980   1985   1990   1995   2000   2005   2010   2015   2020   2025   2030   2035   2040   2045   2050   2055

YVES SAINT LAURENT

The creator of the dinner jacket for women is considered a revolutionary of women's fashion. Together with Christian Dior and Coco Chanel, the Algerian-born Frenchman made Paris the global center of haute couture.

A skeptical gaze and shortsighted eyes protected behind distinctive heavy-framed dark glasses—the trademark of the fashion designer Yves Saint Laurent leaves no room for doubt that this master of couture was in private a shy person. Shyness, alcoholism, drug addiction, and deep depression marked the life of Yves Henri Donat Mathieu Saint Laurent, but did not prevent him from becoming one of the most innovative fashion designers of the twentieth century.

Influenced by his bourgeois mother's passion for fashion, the gentle Saint Laurent soon found the world of textiles a place of refuge—during his schoolboy days from the bullying of his classmates, and later from the whole world. Shortly after his seventeenth birthday he proved his talent for the first time: in 1953 he received the first prize of the International Wool Secretariat for a sketch of a cocktail dress (another competitor at the time was the young Kurt Lagerfeld, see page 70), and only a year later Christian Dior (see page 30) offered him a position in his house. He worked with Dior until his death in 1957, when he was promoted to chief designer—and became an overnight star with his "trapeze line." The Ligne Trapèze at last freed women from the tyranny of the wasp waist, without robbing them of their elegance. Yves Saint Laurent released fashion from padded waists, bosoms, and shoulders, yet still invoked the opulence of early Dior designs.

For three years the "wunderkind of the Paris fashion scene" was in charge at Dior as artistic director, until in 1960 he was drafted for military service in Algeria and was replaced by Dior's former assistant Marc Bohan. Following a series of nervous breakdowns and electric shock treatments, Saint Laurent was discharged after only two months. Despite the brevity of his absence, he was unable to return to his former position as artistic director. Bohan remained in his position as chief designer at Dior. From then

on Saint Laurent, who weighed only ninety pounds on his return, was to numb his anxieties with medications, alcohol, and drugs. And yet his greatest creative period still lay ahead.

Together with his partner in business and life, Pierre Bergé, he founded the fashion house of Yves Saint Laurent Couture (using the compensation payment claimed from his former employer as seed money), and soon afterward, with his Rive Gauche sideline, he invented the principle of commercial prêt-à-porter. With the support of Bergé, a passionate art collector with a marked talent for business management, he would go on to design collections that were to revolutionize classic women's fashions. His Nude Look creations in transparent fabrics caused scandals in the sixties, while his consistent use of

1936 Born in Oran, Algeria, on August 1
1953 Studies at the École de la Chambre Syndicale de la Couture Parisienne
1954–57 Assistant to Christian Dior
1957–61 Chief designer at the house of Dior after the death of Christian Dior
1962 Opens his own fashion house and presents his first collection
1964 Launches his first perfume, Y
1966 Opens a ready-to-wear fashion boutique
1993 The business is taken over by the pharmaceutical company Sanofi
2000 Abandons the creative direction of the ready-to-wear line
2002 Retires from the fashion business
2008 Dies in Paris on June 1

SAINT LAURENT
rive gauche

■ 113 NEW BOND STREET, LONDON W1, 01-493 1800 ■ 33 SLOANE STREET, LONDON SW1, 01-235 6706

left page
A model wearing a pinstripe suit

left
Yves Saint Laurent campaign, 1986/87

above
Yves Saint Laurent, 1977

black—before it became a trend—met with incomprehension (as did his preference for a combination of red and pink). The newly founded fashion house achieved its breakthrough with Op-Art fashion in the style of the artist Piet Mondrian: simply cut shift dresses in white, black, yellow, blue, red, divided into blocks with uncompromisingly strong geometry. With this confirmed success, Saint Laurent turned fashion on its head, above all with cuts that until then had been reserved for men's clothing (his women's tuxedo of 1966 was so successful that it is consistently reinterpreted even today). Of his later collections, his innovative "safari look" and the looks inspired by Russian folklore stand out.

In 2002 Saint Laurent announced his retirement from fashion, living in seclusion in Paris up to his death. The legacy of this shy genius is more than 5,000 dresses and 15,000 accessories and sketches, which are being preserved for posterity, at a constant temperature and 50 percent humidity, at the Fondation Pierre Bergé-Yves Saint Laurent.

Farah Diba, empress of Iran, and
Yves Saint Laurent at a fitting, 1959

1888 First issue of the *Financial Times*

1913 George Bernard Shaw
publishes *Pygmalion*

1945 Founding of the United Nations

1900 Boxer Rebellion in China

1929 In the U.K. women are granted
the vote from the age of 21

1959 Miles Davis
leases the a
Kind of Blue

| 1880 | 1885 | 1890 | 1895 | 1900 | 1905 | 1910 | 1915 | 1920 | 1925 | 1930 | 1935 | 1940 | 1945 | 1950 | 1955 | 1960 | 1965 |

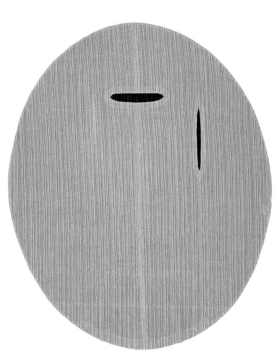

Rhythm Pleats:
left: Exhibition *Enerigeen*,
Stedelijk Museum, Amsterdam, 1990
Photo: Anzaï
right: Rhythm Pleats, 1989
Photo: Yasuaki Yoshinaga

ISSEY MIYAKE

Origami on the body. Issey Miyake creates body sculptures, combining influences from East and West into a gesamtkunstwerk.

In Japanese, Issey means "a life" and Miyake "three houses." Fitting, for the Japanese designer's style reflects more than one influence. After graduating from the Tama Art University in 1964 with a degree in graphic design, Miyake studied and apprenticed in Paris and New York, before returning to Tokyo to start his own company. Issey Miyake has created a world of fashion that links art, technology, and tradition. He had already become interested in textiles, producing *A Poem in Fabric and Stone*, in which he reflects upon clothing as a "visual phenomenon." In 1965 he moved to Paris to study at the École de la Chambre Syndicale de la Couture Parisienne. It was during this time in Paris that he experienced first-hand the student unrest: "All this striving for freedom, the openness, the discussions, fascinated me." He began to eschew the elitist quality of couture and began to think toward more universal clothing like the jeans and T-shirts sported by the students, which would suit the needs of all people.

In order to win a place in the fashion world with his designs, in 1970 Miyake returned to Japan to establish the Miyake Design Studio in Tokyo. There, for over thirty years he and his team have turned out creations he describes as "80 percent." The remaining 20 percent, according to Miyake, is left to the wearer. She has the final say on how to wear the garment. The other thing these adjustable works have in common is the understanding, shaped by Eastern thought, that the fabric (for Miyake there is no material which cannot serve for the production of clothing) is central to the design, as a protective covering. Instead of following the lines of the body, his designs break through this silhouette. Thus for Miyake the body—in contrast to his Western designer colleagues—is not the

motif, but merely the medium of his textile art. The result is that in his clothes, constructed from circular and rectangular pieces of fabric, every woman becomes a geometrical figure. The space between the cloth and body and how they interact with one another becomes the point of interest.

Since the early nineties, Miyake, who continually develops his concepts rather than working from season to season, has been intensely occupied with the Japanese tradition of pleating material. With his "Pleats Please" collection, still in existence, he revived the technique for the twentieth century, though using state-of-the-art technology. The clothing, mostly made in ultra-light polyester fabrics, gains its form in a manner different than regular pleated fabrics, which are cut and sewn after the fabric has been pleated. In Miyake's revolutionary process, the fabric is cut and sewn first into whatever shape he desires, then pleated using a heat-press to retain the pleats in the fabric's memory. The fabrics, often pleated diagonally, not only enclose the wearer's body in concertina fashion, but also always retain their form, even in a crumpled state.

In 1998, Issey Miyake returned to his first love, research and experimentation, with a new collection to be entitled "A-POC (A Piece Of Cloth)." The earliest evolutions of A-POC were clothing that was mass-produced and that could later be finished by the wearer, customized to suit her whims. It later developed beyond this into more complex woven materials and techniques using an industrial knitting or weaving machine harnessed to a computer. The preliminary step of making a sketch is omitted, and no material is wasted. The co-developer of the project is Dai Fujiwara, who in 2007 rose to become the creative director of the Issey Miyake line.

1938 Born in Hiroshima on April 22
1970 Establishes the *MIYAKE DESIGN STUDIO* in Tokyo
1971 First overseas collection is shown in New York
1973 Participates in the Paris Autumn Winter '73 Collections
1983/1985 Presents the exhibition *Issey Miyake Spectacle: Body-works* in Tokyo, Los Angeles, San Francisco, and London
1988 Starts experimenting with pleating
1993 Launches *PLEATS PLEASE ISSEY MIYAKE*
1998 Embarks upon the A-POC project
1998–2000 Presents the exhibition *ISSEY MIYAKE MAKING THINGS* in Paris, New York, and Tokyo
2006 Opens 21_21 DESIGN SIGHT in Tokyo and is appointed as one of its directors

left
A-POC Kanazawa, 2004
Photo: Marcus Tomlinson

above
Mr. Miyake portrait
Photo: Yuriko Takagi

ROD STEIGER

1929 Erich Maria Remarque publishes
All Quiet on the Western Front

1898 Pierre and Marie Curie
discover radium

1954–62 Algerian War

1916 In the Battle of Verdun, more than
700,000 German and French soldiers
are killed or wounded

1943 Premiere of *Casablanca*, directed
by Michael Curtiz

1887–89 The Eiffel Tower constructed in Paris

| 1880 | 1885 | 1890 | 1895 | 1900 | 1905 | 1910 | 1915 | 1920 | 1925 | 1930 | 1935 | 1940 | 1945 | 1950 | 1955 | 1960 | 1965 |

Claudia Schiffer in a black tweed suit
from the spring/summer 1995 haute
couture collection

1979 Second oil crisis   **1991** Boris Yeltsin becomes the first democratically
elected president of Russia

The Roman Curia abolishes the *Index of
Prohibited Books*, in vigor since 1559   **2003** U.S. invasion of Iraq

| 1970 | 1975 | 1980 | 1985 | 1990 | 1995 | 2000 | 2005 | 2010 | 2015 | 2020 | 2025 | 2030 | 2035 | 2040 | 2045 | 2050 | 2055 |

KARL LAGERFELD

Karl the Great: the German successor to Chanel is among the most important designers of the twentieth century.

Anything that can be said about Karl Lagerfeld has already been said elsewhere and probably more accurately by the fashion designer himself. In order to describe the entire range of his achievements, one would need to use as many words in each line as the master himself utters per minute when speaking. For the eloquent designer with the occasionally acid tongue designs not only fashion (at the rate of some twenty collections a year), accessories, and diverse lifestyle products, he also supplies costumes for operas and films, collects art, designs sets, illustrates, photographs, writes, and publishes—all at the same time. If the term "workaholic" did not exist, it would have to be invented for Lagerfeld. It is a matter of discipline. Quite unusually for the industry, the designer steers clear of alcohol, cigarettes, drugs, even sugar and prolonged periods of sleep. His strength of will, meanwhile, is almost more famous than the superb wit and almost inexhaustible knowledge with which he peppers his numerous interviews. Even if the French long ago adopted the cosmopolitan German as one of their own (even though he rarely makes kind references to his adoptive compatriots), the Hamburg-born Lagerfeld remains loyal to Prussian principles. Otherwise he could hardly accommodate all his creative activity within a single life.

According to his own account, Lagerfeld was born in 1938 (other sources say 1933) in well-to-do circumstances. As a teenager he moved with his mother to Paris, where in 1954 he received the first prize of the International Wool Secretariat for a coat design. This was followed by a three-year apprenticeship in couture with Pierre Balmain (see page 38), and then a position as artistic director at Jean Patou. Lagerfeld became increasingly interested in prêt-à-porter, which he found fresher and more appropriate to the times. In 1963 he became a freelance designer, but in the same year he signed up with the fashion house Chloé, where he was twice chief designer, in 1963–83

and 1993–97. Since 1965 he has also designed fur collections for the Italian fashion house Fendi. Later Lagerfeld was also active in the mass production of ready-to-wear, as evidenced by his designs for Steilmann (1987–95), the mail-order business Quelle (1996), and the Swedish clothing giant H&M in 2004.

In 1983 he received an offer to take over the artistic direction at Chanel. Lagerfeld seized the opportunity, although the house had decidedly lost its direction since the death of its founder Coco Chanel (see page 20) in 1971, and indeed was threatening to sink into obscurity. The industry doubted whether Lagerfeld could bring new life to the aging "Chanel style." These doubts were soon cast aside. Since his debut on Rue Cambon, the designer has consistently reinterpreted the stylistic heritage of his predecessor, always in a contemporary fashion, by concentrating on the essence of the label and continually updating its aesthetic. In spite of his myriad interests, at Chanel Lagerfeld exhibits enormous staying power. He rejuvenates and transforms with irony rather than blatantly imitating the founder's look. And rather than using all elements of the Chanel style at once, Lagerfeld deploys a vocabulary of pearls, diamond patterns, gold chains, tweed (often in pink or pale green), camellias, and the famous "double C," which he uses in almost provocative exaggeration in his collections. With Lagerfeld, hotpants are matched with bouclé, knitted jackets worn with biker boots, and microminis combined with baroque pearls the size of golf balls.

In order to achieve that perfect Chanel image, Lagerfeld not only personally conceives and takes photographs for his ad campaigns, he also turns to the charms of one of his many muses (including Inès de la Fressange, Claudia Schiffer, Stella Tennant, Devon Aoki, Nicole Kidman, and Lily Allen), which he alternates according to the zeitgeist. And while it may seem at times that Lagerfeld is the creator and

1938 Born in Hamburg on September 10
1958–63 Assistant, later artistic director at Jean Patou
1963–84 Chief designer for the house of Chloé
FROM 1964 Independent fashion designer for various fashion houses
1975 Launches his first perfume
FROM 1983 Chief designer of haute couture and prêt-à-porter for the house of Chanel
1984 Founds his own label
FROM 1986 Active as a fashion photographer
1998 Opens the Lagerfeld Gallery in Paris
2004 Collection for Hennes & Mauritz (H&M)

Karl Lagerfeld, 2009

guarantor of the success of the Chanel look, he would not be Lagerfeld if he concentrated only on the prestige of his employer. This couturier is a master of skillful self-presentation and has transformed himself into his own trademark, with a powder-white ponytail and his ever-present sunglasses and fan. At the beginning of the new millennium he exchanged the fan for fingerless gloves, heavy necklaces (on which among other things hang his parents' wedding rings), and high-neck collars. Within a year he shed more than ninety pounds as a publicity stunt to fit into the slim-cut Dior suits of his young designer colleague Hedi Slimane (see page 142). For when he discovers outstanding talent, he does not shrink from encouraging it—even in that exceptional case when it happens not to be his own.

see page 142

left page
Natalia Vodianova in a ruched blouse
stand-up collar, fall/winter 2003/04
haute couture collection

left
New interpretation of the "little black dress" in the fall/winter 2005/06 prêt-à-porter collection

above
Spring/summer 2008 prêt-à-porter collection

RALPH LAUREN

WOODY ALLEN

BOB DYLAN

1929 First presentation of the Academy
Awards, known as the Oscars

1955 First documenta exhib
in Kassel

1895 First public film screening
in Berlin

1912 The *Titanic* sinks in the North Atlantic

1939 The German Wehrmacht marches
into Poland on September 1

1880 1885 1890 1895 1900 1905 1910 1915 1920 1925 1930 1935 1940 1945 1950 1955 1960 1965

Tweed ensemble from the fall 2009 collection

1970 Fall of the Chilean president
Salvador Allende

1994 Nelson Mandela becomes first black
president of South Africa

1983 Production of the first
commercial cell phone

2007 Al Gore receives the Nobel Peace Prize

2001 War in Afghanistan begins

1970 1975 1980 1985 1990 1995 2000 2005 2010 2015 2020 2025 2030 2035 2040 2045 2050 2055

RALPH LAUREN

The pioneer of American style makes "fashion for people who actually don't want to be fashionable."

It started with a simple necktie—colorful, wide, and in a college style—just like the ones that had been so immensely popular in the 1970s. Its creator had borrowed $50,000 in order to open his tie shop, Polo Fashions, in New York. It proved a good investment. For what began more than forty years ago with a small collection of ties is today a lifestyle empire, exporting the American Dream in the form of fabric to the rest of the world. But the secret of Ralph Lauren's success is a straightforward one. He was quite simply the first designer to give Americans what they had long desired—a style of their own.

His birthplace, not a promising one for a fashion designer, was the Bronx, hardly the most glamorous borough of New York City. Born the son of a Belorussian Jewish immigrant shortly after the out-break of World War II in modest circumstances, the diminutive boy with the ice-blue eyes soon knew where he wanted to go: to the top. Knowing it was up to himself to acquire the fine charms of wealth ("All I had was taste!"), by the age of sixteen he dropped his family name, Lifschitz (it was the little syllable "shit" that bothered him), and called himself by the more American-sounding name Lauren. Already as a teenager he worked as an assistant in a menswear shop, while regularly investing his pay in custom-made suits. In 1967, after a few years as a student of economics, a soldier in the U.S. army, and a salesman at Brooks Brothers, he went into business in Manhattan, selling those same wide neckties.

A stunning success, he soon launched his first complete men's collection, and his first collection for women followed in the early seventies. His style was a small revolution: Lauren ignored the hippie look and roundly rejected polyester despite its popularity in the fashion industry. Instead, for his designs he followed his own dream. The result was a dandyish "Ivy League chic," coupled with early-American legend and an aristocratic English style.

Pinstripes are paired with tweed and heavy knit cashmere, denim shirts with cowboy boots and Western pants, safari shirts with linen chinos. The basic principles have hardly changed. Lauren is the grand master of American casual fused with a touch of European elegance. This self-made billionaire does not just design fashion, nor does he wish to set trends. Rather, Lauren, a marketing strategist, creates worlds of exaggerated perfection that paradoxically come across as authentic to the last detail. Ralph Lauren's clients do not wear their preferred label, they live it. It is no wonder, since his brand has broadly diversified. In addition to a dozen different men's and women's labels, Ralph Lauren also creates children's fashions and athletic wear, bestowing upon American sportswear in the nineties nothing short of its own identity. And there is more—from cosmetics to wall paint, he designs all the accessories for what his critics mockingly call a "Laurenized" life.

Lauren's omnipresent polo-player figure was intro-duced as early as 1971, when he showed his first women's collection. This striking figure of a sports-man rapidly became the distinctive trademark of the preppies and their families, and later the yuppies of the eighties. Today, the riding figure remains unchallenged as a seal of quality for classic American sporting chic.

It was not only with his logo that Ralph Lauren put his money on the right horse. This son of a Russian immigrant is now not only the most successful, but also the most American of all U.S. fashion designers. A father of three and passionate collector of classic cars, he has, however, to this day never become a polo player.

1939 Born in New York on October 12
as Ralph Lifschitz
1967 Founds the label with a line of
neckties
1968 Designs his first men's collection
1971 Designs his first women's
collection
1978 Launch of the first perfume for
women, Lauren for Women,
and the first perfume for men,
Polo for Men
1981 Becomes first U.S. designer to
open a flagship store in Europe
(New Bond Street, London)
1997 The label becomes a publicly
owned company
2006–10 Official outfitter of
Wimbledon

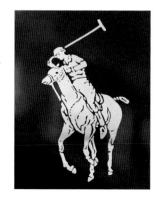

right
Polo Logo

above
Ralph Lauren, 1986

1890 End of the Indian Wars in the U.S.   **1914** Opening of the Panama Canal

1903 The U.S. leases Guantánamo Bay,   **1930** Constantinople   **1960** Forming of
Cuba, as a naval base for 99 years   renamed Istanbul   The Beatle

1945 Beginning of the Cold War

| 1880 | 1885 | 1890 | 1895 | 1900 | 1905 | 1910 | 1915 | 1920 | 1925 | 1930 | 1935 | 1940 | 1945 | 1950 | 1955 | 1960 | 1965 |

KENZO

Harrods . London . www.kenzo.com

Kenzo campaign, 2009

1972–74 The North Tower of the World Trade
Center is the world's tallest building

1998 Michel Houellebecq publishes
The Elementary Particles

1985 Live Aid charity concert
in aid of Africa

2008 Escalation of the Caucasus conflict
between Russia and Georgia

1970　1975　1980　1985　1990　1995　2000　2005　2010　2015　2020　2025　2030　2035　2040　2045　2050　2055

KENZO TAKADA

The master of the ethnic look, since the 1970s the label of Japanese Kenzo Takada has presented a unique folkloric mix uniting styles from all over the world.

On a June morning in 1994, Parisians woke up to find one of their famous landmarks, the Pont Neuf, covered in flowers. Thousands of begonias blossomed on walls and pillars—a bright splash of color created by the Japanese designer Kenzo Takada, who had arrived to the French capital in 1965. It took only a few years for him to make his mark with a style that at the time had no official name in the fashion world: the "ethnic look." His idea of combining in his collections colors, patterns, cuts, and style elements from all over the world was sensational. He spread merriment with the creation of a tweed kimono, checkered sarongs, and flowered peasant skirts. It was well known that at a Kenzo show even the models smiled.

Kenzo's start in the city of fashion, however, was far from rosy. The twenty-six-year-old had little money, knew no one, and spoke not a word of French. But this diminutive man with the shoulder-length hair was not one to give up easily. Born in 1939 in Himeji, against his parents' wishes he enrolled in the well-known Bunka Fashion College in Tokyo, one of the first males to do so. He next embarked on a six-week sea journey to reach Paris. It took him five years to raise the money to open his first boutique. He rented the shop in the Galerie Vivienne around the corner from the Palais Royal, renovating and decorating it inspired by the jungle paintings of Henri Rousseau. In 1970 Jungle Jap opened its doors and Kenzo showed his first collection with fabrics bought at bargain prices from a nearby market.
Jungle Jap soon became the favorite label of young, fashionable models. Around the world people were on a spiritual journey and the hippie style was all the rage. Kenzo regularly put on small presentations, made new contacts, and was overwhelmed by success. He sent out 700 invitations for his "Jap Fashion Show" and more than 2,000 Kenzo fans turned up. His seamstresses could no longer keep

up with the flood of orders. And what was more, his designs were being copied everywhere.
With his thriving, innovative "ethnic style" Kenzo proved to the Paris fashion scene that even a non-Frenchman could build up and direct a French fashion house. In 1999, to the great astonishment of the fashion industry, the designer announced his retirement. Since 2003 the Sardinian Antonio Marras, now artistic director of the house, has been quite successful continuing what Kenzo Takada began in 1970: a stylistic, multicolor journey around the world.

1939 Born in Hyogo, Japan, on
February 27
1958 Begins study at Bunka Fashion
College in Tokyo
1965 Moves to Paris
1970 Presents his first collection and
opens first boutique
1983 Launches a men's collection
1988 Launch of his first perfume, Kenzo
1993 Sale of the business to the luxury
goods business LVMH
1999 Retires as artistic director of the
fashion house
SINCE 2005 Presents several table-
ware, decorative, and furniture
lines under the new label Gokan
Kobo

above
Kenzo Takada

following pages
Dramatic evening gown from the
spring/summer 2007 collection

AZZEDINE ALAÏA

ELVIS PRESLEY

JEFF WALL

1915–17 Armenian Genocide in the Ottoman Empire

1943 Antoine de Saint-Exupéry publishes
The Little Prince

1885 Karl Benz builds the first
automobile with a gasoline
engine

1901 Norway becomes the first European
country to introduce women's suffrage
on a local level

1929 Opening of the Museum of
Modern Art in New York

1961 Forming of t
Beach Boys

1880 1885 1890 1895 1900 1905 1910 1915 1920 1925 1930 1935 1940 1945 1950 1955 1960 1965

Grace Jones at a fitting with
Azzedine Alaïa, 1977

1973 First oil crisis

1998 The Lewinsky affair becomes public

1983 Discovery of the HIV virus

2007 Assassination of Pakistani
politician Benazir Bhutto

1970   1975   1980   1985   1990   1995   2000   2005   2010   2015   2020   2025   2030   2035   2040   2045   2050   2055

AZZEDINE ALAÏA

Tight, tighter, skintight: since the 1980s he has been the "King of Cling."

He prefers to wear black satin Chinese jackets, dark velvet slippers, and loose-fitting pants. His creations, on the other hand, fit like a second skin and define every curve—in Azzedine Alaïa's clothes every woman becomes a living sculpture. Not surprising, since it was sculpture the Tunisian-born designer had originally studied.

During his studies at the École des Beaux Arts in Tunis, Alaïa observed the human body in detail. After graduating, he decided to pay homage to it in soft fabric rather than carve it from cold stone. While still studying, a dressmaker schooled him in the art of sewing. And with her he reworked the patterns from Paris fashion magazines. A short time later he was living in the city of fashion. In 1957, Alaïa, born the son of a simple wheat farmer, was given a job by the couture legend Christian Dior (see page 30)—albeit leaving the label after only a few days. His next positions, with Guy Laroche and Thierry Mugler (see page 102), did, however, last for a couple of seasons. Yet it was his job as housekeeper and personal tailor to the Comtesse de Blégiers that gave the later star couturier his first chance to realize his own designs. His employer's house was frequented by the elite of Paris society, for whom he was soon to begin designing.

Finally, in 1980, a patent leather coat, perforated and adorned with studs, gave him his international breakthrough. Five years later he presented to the world his now unmistakable style: he designed a magenta-colored latex dress—so severely laced it was skintight—for the flamboyant performer Grace Jones. It looked as though the designer had transformed pure sex into fabric. Secure in his success, from then on he enclosed women's bodies in lycra, latex, stretch fabric, and leather. His unique selling point was that, despite maximum definition of the body, his clothes, often bias-cut, allowed the wearer to experience the greatest possible freedom of movement.

Today Alaïa's creations are less extreme. And yet his designs are still based on the body rather than trends. Although the adoptive Parisian loves fashion, he doesn't see himself as part of the fashion industry. He presents his creations outside the fashion calendar, at small shows in his own home, over tea and cakes, with no press in sight: "I make fashion because I love fashion, and not in order to put on a show." He believes collections with fixed deadlines to be a "commercial hell that has nothing to do with creativity." Alaïa refuses to "throw his fashion mindlessly onto the market like his colleagues." Instead, he designs directly for his exclusive client base, or for occasions that pique his interest. Which actually makes sense—after all, an artist does not produce his works according to a calendar.

1940 Born in Jemmal, Tunisia, on June 7
BEFORE 1957 Studies sculpture at the École des Beaux-Arts in Tunis
1957 Moves to Paris
1957–70 Assistant to various designers including Christian Dior, Guy Laroche, and Thierry Mugler
1970 Opens haute couture studio in Paris
1980 Presents his first prêt-à-porter collection
1988 Opens boutiques in Paris, New York, and Beverly Hills
2000 Sells business to Prada
2007 Buys business back from Prada

Azzedine Alaïa, 2008

1892 First issue of American *Vogue*

1918 U.S. president Wilson presents
his Fourteen Points program

1945 Marilyn Monroe discovered
as photo model

1961 Founding c
Amnesty
Internatio

1905 Constitutional Revolution in Iran

1931–72 The Empire State Building in New York
is the tallest building in the world

1880 1885 1890 1895 1900 1905 1910 1915 1920 1925 1930 1935 1940 1945 1950 1955 1960 1965

Vivienne Westwood at the end of her
spring/summer 2010 prêt-à-porter show
in Paris, October 2009

| 1973 | Premiere of Richard O'Brien's *The Rocky Horror Show* | 1995 | Founding of the World Trade Organization (WTO) |
| 1983 | Pope John Paul II rehabilitates Galileo Galilei | 2004 | Murder of Dutch film director Theo van Gogh |

1970   1975   1980   1985   1990   1995   2000   2005   2010   2015   2020   2025   2030   2035   2040   2045   2050   2055

VIVIENNE WESTWOOD

This British designer is considered the mother of punk. Today she is bourgeois, but her anarchistic attitude remains.

"I used to believe that there was a door to kick down, but now I know it's not there at all. There are just jumps along the way," says the inventor of punk style Vivienne Westwood these days. There is no more appropriate way of describing her biography—for hardly anyone has developed as consistently as this provocative British designer, who despite all "jumps" has succeeded in preserving her ideals.

Westwood was at first an elementary school teacher and, it is said, a very committed one. But her creativity and radical sympathies soon encouraged her to make a break in her career. In the early seventies, together with the art student and later manager of the Sex Pistols, Malcolm McLaren, she opened a small boutique on London's King's Road. In the mid-seventies, after several name changes and different themes—from rock 'n' roll to fetish sex—the store became the mecca of a lost generation then developing into an anti-hippie subculture. Seditionaries, Westwood's boutique, became the nucleus of punk.

Instead of first-graders, Westwood was now educating her customers—to adopt a look that expressed their frustration with unemployment, lack of educational possibilities, and recession. Without seeing herself as a designer, Westwood created clothes that were to decidedly influence the new punk style. Her first creations were mainly based on ready-to-wear fashion, which she tore to pieces, tied up, and decorated with provocative slogans (or sometimes fake urine stains). This radically slapdash look was completed with sewn-up zippers, safety pins, rivets, steel chains, and chicken bones. Then, in the late seventies, something happened to punk that eventually happens to all avant-garde movements: it was appropriated by the bourgeois mainstream. And Vivienne Westwood? She prepared herself for the next big jump. She no longer sought her inspiration in the street, but in the museum. Westwood, the archetypal self-taught genius,

began to take historical costumes to pieces in order to understand how they were made. The result was ever more complex creations, which she began showing in the mid-eighties at Paris Fashion Week.

The subculture rebel has now become a fashion designer of worldwide renown. Characteristic of the new Westwood look are items from the history of fashion, combined with provocative topical themes. Among her trademarks are tweed fabrics, platform heels, and above all a form of femininity, old-fashioned in its use of corsages and crinolines, but in a fresh way, which makes of women powerful sexual creatures rather than sex objects.

1941   Born in Tintwistle, England, on April 8
1959   Trains as an elementary school teacher
1970   Opens her first boutique with Malcolm McLaren on King's Road in London
1981   Presents her first collection, "Pirate," in London
1992   Presents her first prêt-à-porter collection
1996   Costume design for a production of *The Threepenny Opera* by Bertolt Brecht and Kurt Weill at the Burgtheater in Vienna
1998   Creates her first perfume, Boudoir
1999   Opens her first U.S. flagship store in New York

left
Taffeta suit from the fall/winter 2009 collection

above
Vivienne Westwood, 2009

And although England's favorite eccentric has become bourgeois, she is still a rebel. A daughter of the working class, with her enduring independence as a businesswoman she above all challenges the continuing march of the capitalization and commercialization of today's fashion industry. For only she who is free can decide where the next jump will take her.

Presentation of the fall/winter 2009/10 collection

1908 In Detroit, the first Ford automobile, the Model T, rolls off the assembly line

1931 Founding of the Whitney Museum of American Art in New York

1922 The tomb of the pharaoh Tutankhamen discovered in the Valley of the Kings

1946–54 Indochina War

1958 Truman Capote publishes *Breakfast at Tiffany's*

1894–95 First Sino-Japanese War

1880	1885	1890	1895	1900	1905	1910	1915	1920	1925	1930	1935	1940	1945	1950	1955	1960	1965

Model Natalia Vodianova in a white slip dress from the spring 2003 collection

1971 Founding of Greenpeace

1993 Eritrea becomes the last African country to declare independence

1979 Second oil crisis

2004 The Abu Ghraib torture scandal becomes public

1970 · 1975 · 1980 · 1985 · 1990 · 1995 · 2000 · 2005 · 2010 · 2015 · 2020 · 2025 · 2030 · 2035 · 2040 · 2045 · 2050 · 2055

CALVIN KLEIN

The American designer made jeans provocative and put simple white underwear back on the map. His fashion formed the basis of American "Clean Chic."

"You wanna know what comes between me and my Calvins? Nothing." With this provocative confession by the then-adolescent Brooke Shields in the mid-seventies, Calvin Klein scandalized the public to great effect: the lucrative by-product of his calculated move amounted to several hundred thousand of those "Calvins" (actually nothing more than simple, dark-blue drainpipe jeans) flying off America's shelves at record speed. With his campaign, the designer had discovered his personal formula for success, according to which conspicuous marketing is often just as important as the clothing itself. And nothing has changed since then.

Calvin Richard Klein was born to Hungarian-Jewish immigrants in the Bronx. While his parents earned their meager income, his grandmother taught the boy to sew. After leaving school Klein studied for two years at the Fashion Institute of Technology, after which he designed for a few years for Dan Misstein, a large American coat manufacturer. In 1968, at the age of twenty-six, Klein was finally prepared to realize his dream of independence and the financial success that accompanied it. With a loan of a mere $10,000 as starting capital, together with his childhood friend, Barry Schwartz, he founded the firm of Calvin Klein Ltd.

The fashion he created in the early seventies was still strongly influenced by the work of his designer colleagues in Paris—not unusual in America at that point. Over time, however, Klein found his own striking style. Simple lines combined with high-quality natural materials—cashmere, suede, cotton, and tweed—in muted colors, soon earned him the title bestowed on him by the American press: "Supreme Master of Minimalism." Klein's tailoring is formfitting, straight-lined, and unisex, with women's fashions strongly oriented towards the men's.

Klein was immediately successful, but his big commercial breakthrough only came with his very personal strategy. More than just simply putting a naked Brooke Shields into blue drainpipe jeans, his calculated breach of taboo was complemented by a clever idea: instead of being covered by the waistband, Klein's label was conspicuously displayed on the seat pocket. The "nameless" jeans became desirable brand goods. With his label on the outside of the garment, Klein became the initiator of an era known today as the cult of the label, which found its high point in the logomania of the nineties. With his next project Klein once again delivered provocation, naked skin, and brand visibility. The product in question? Simple white cotton underwear for men to which Klein attached a plain stretch waistband imprinted with the brand name. Klein had not reinvented male undergarments, regardless of what the reaction (worldwide hysteria and mass consumption) might lead one to believe. It was not the design that transformed the product from an everyday article of clothing into a status symbol, but rather the brand image and the power of that image. Bruce Weber photographed the rapper and later Hollywood actor Mark Wahlberg—then better known as Marky Mark—with his washboard stomach and his hand on his crotch, clad only in white "Calvin" briefs. These provocative images are today among the most memorable and successful campaigns in advertising history.

In 2003 Calvin Klein sold his firm (or rather empire, which covers nearly every area of fashion and lifestyle) to the U.S. shirt company Phillips-Van Heusen, signing on as a consultant until 2011.

1942 Born in New York on November 19
1960–62 Studies at the Fashion Institute of Technology in New York
1968 Founds his own fashion house with Barry Schwartz
1979 Sensational advertising campaign featuring Brooke Shields in Calvin Klein jeans with the tagline "Nothing comes between me and my Calvins"
1982 Launch of men's underwear line
1985 Launch of his first perfume, Obsession
1995 Steven Gaines and Sharon Churcher publish the biography *Obsession: The Lives and Times of Calvin Klein*
2003 Sale of business to Philips-Van Heusen and retirement from the fashion business

left
"Marky" Mark Wahlberg, 1995

above
Calvin Klein, 2009

Calvin Klein advertisement displayed on a New York City bus in August 1995. The advertising campaign, which appeared in print and on television, sparked a national controversy because of its perceived resemblance to child pornography.

1900 Derivation of radiation law
by Max Planck

1931 Japan occupies
Northeast China

1953 Coronation of Queen
Elizabeth II in London's
Westminster Abbey

1893 First performance of Antonín Dvořák's   **1914–18** World War I
Ninth Symphony (*From the New World*)

1941 Premiere of Orson Welles' film
Citizen Kane

| 1880 | 1885 | 1890 | 1895 | 1900 | 1905 | 1910 | 1915 | 1920 | 1925 | 1930 | 1935 | 1940 | 1945 | 1950 | 1955 | 1960 | 1965 |

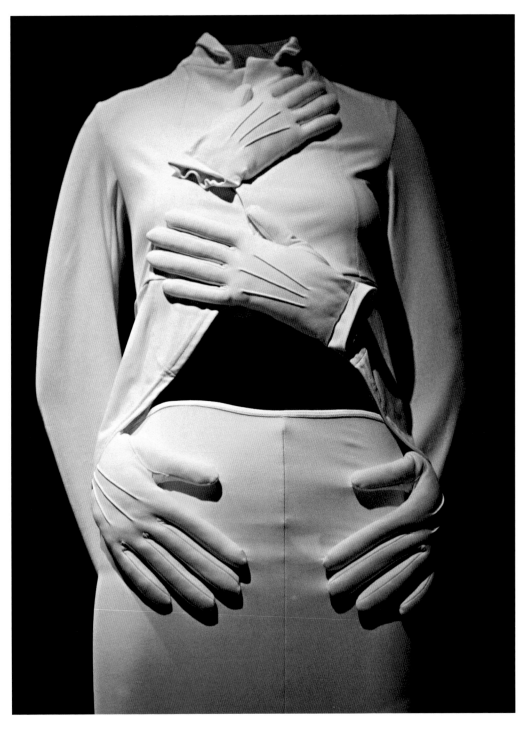

Rei Kawakubo's designs on
display at the *blog.mode:
addressing fashion* exhibition at
the Metropolitan Museum of
Art in New York, December 2007

6–73 Construction of the World
Trade Center in New York

1992 Maastricht Treaty founds the
European Union (EU)

1977 Attacks by left-wing extremists
Baader-Meinhof Group (Red Army
Faction) in West Germany

2004 Founding of the online social
network Facebook

| 1970 | 1975 | 1980 | 1985 | 1990 | 1995 | 2000 | 2005 | 2010 | 2015 | 2020 | 2025 | 2030 | 2035 | 2040 | 2045 | 2050 | 2055 |

REI KAWAKUBO

In the 1980s, this Japanese designer turned the Western ideal of beauty on its head, to lasting effect. Her fashion stands for intellectual constructivism and experimental silhouettes, consciously distancing itself from classical styling.

Rei Kawakubo, Japanese fashion designer and founder of the couture house Comme des Garçons, does not care much for convention. Rather, by her own admission, she likes to question the status quo. So it is not surprising that her European debut (a ready-to-wear collection shown during Paris Fashion Week 1981) landed like a bomb in the midst of the hype-filled glamour world of the eighties.

The models who crept along the Comme des Garçons catwalk seemed unprepossessing by the standards of the day, disheveled, with uncombed hair, and unmade-up apart from rouge slapped almost at random on their faces. Their feet were clad in flats and their bodies enveloped in a barely decorative manner in grey-black tunics with rope belts and pullovers apparently deliberately full of holes (Kawakubo had loosened the screws of her knitting machines to achieve this effect). What the designer delivered that evening in Paris was nothing less than a challenge to all standards of beauty, unmasking the concept of woman as a graceful, beautiful creature as a mere social construct: classic fashion, just like beauty, is no more than a perishable good.

Kawakubo, then barely forty and an established star in her own country, was issuing a challenge to the Western fashion world, which was not slow to reply. The trade press unreflectingly attacked the collection as "post-nuclear rag-picker fashion," "Quasimodo style," and "apocalyptic end-of-the-world fashion." The industry itself perceived the designs as impertinent, whose effect however was not to be underestimated. A year later, the mainstream collections of her designer colleagues included items with rags and holes.

Kawakubo's design philosophy has not changed, except that in the meantime her colleagues have come to understand that her fashion is not to be understood as a mere social affront. Fashion is not disguise, but finds its form for its own sake, freed

from a beautiful (but superficial) existence. Her designs play with imperfection, are timeless, and allow the wearer space for imagination. Her garments are sometimes oversized and inflated, strongly marked by asymmetries and layering. In contrast to Western fashion oriented to the body, either exaggerating or negating it, the Japanese designer continually finds her own, novel forms—in her fashion the human being is more than a mere silhouette.

Kawakubo's approach to fashion may be due to her career trajectory. Born in Tokyo in 1942, self-taught, she studied art and literature, until she designed her first items of clothing in 1969. In 1972 she called her label, which she still runs independently, Comme des Garçons, meaning "like the boys." As early as the seventies she began to present her fashion in a minimalist, cool interior, like objects in a gallery. Clothing should not be perceived as goods, but as part of a total concept, whose value is only highlighted by the almost extravagant use of open space. Today, while her competitors are following the same path of flagship stores marked by a corporate identity, Kawakubo has decisively changed the concept. Her fashions are sold in so-called "guerrilla stores," in rented temporary premises, and move house after a year.

Rei Kawakubo's uncompromising approach is refreshingly demanding in the starkly commercial world of fashion. With Comme des Garçons she shows that success can be achieved without glossing over one's vision. She herself, incidentally, is not so sure. "There are two kinds of people: some do what they believe in, and compromise as little as possible; for the rest, only profit counts. These people are gaining more and more power. I am fighting against this, although I know that in the end I can't win."

1942 Born in Tokyo on October 11
1964 Completes art studies at Keio
University in Tokyo
1964–67 Works in the marketing
department of a large chemical
organization
FROM 1967 Independent fashion
designer
1972 Founds her own fashion house,
Comme des Garçons
1975 Opens her first flagship store
in Tokyo
1978 Introduces a men's line
1981 First presentation of collections
at the Paris fashion shows
1994 Launch of her first perfume,
Comme des Garçons
1992 Gives up the creative direction
of her fashion house
2008 Creation of a fashion collection
for the Swedish fashion house
H&M and a handbag collection
for Louis Vuitton

Rei Kawakubo

1900 L. Frank Baum publishes
The Wizard of Oz

1922–53 Josef Stalin is general secretary of the
Communist Party of the Soviet Union

1947 UN partition plan for Palestine

1887 Heinrich Hertz produces first artificial
electromagnetic waves

1910 The first film producers
settle in Hollywood

1937–45 Second Sino-Japanese
War

1880 1885 1890 1895 1900 1905 1910 1915 1920 1925 1930 1935 1940 1945 1950 1955 1960 1965

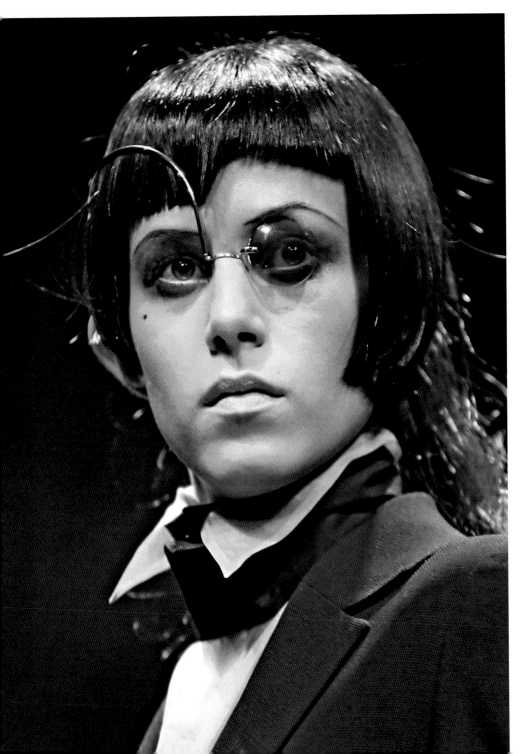

Look of the spring/summer 2007
prêt-à-porter collection

Forming of the group
Pink Floyd

1992–95 Bosnian War

2007 Romania and Bulgaria accepted
as members of the EU

1976 Apple Computer, Inc. is founded

| 1970 | 1975 | 1980 | 1985 | 1990 | 1995 | 2000 | 2005 | 2010 | 2015 | 2020 | 2025 | 2030 | 2035 | 2040 | 2045 | 2050 | 2055 |

YOHJI YAMAMOTO

In the early 1980s this avant-garde designer's deconstructed clothes turned the Western idea of aesthetics on its head.

His premiere in Paris produced an outcry: the dismayed fashion establishment called the garments from the Japanese designer's 1981 Western debut "Hiroshima Chic." Yohji Yamamoto radically broke with the then dominant aesthetic. He showed neither padded power shoulders, nor miniskirts, nor high heels; instead his models, their faces in white make-up, wore black asymmetrical clothing and flats. The dazzling femme fatale of the eighties was suddenly confronted with her counterpart—an intellectual, androgynous creature with a crow-like silhouette seemingly from another world. Yohji Yamamoto created not just a new look, but a whole new approach to fashion whose effect on cuts and forms can still be seen today. And to which he has always remained faithful.

"You can say that designing is quite easy; the difficulty lies in finding a new way to explore beauty," Yohji Yamamoto once said. The key word for his fashion is deconstruction. He systematically takes the Western tradition of tailoring apart without disrespecting it. He moves seams, shifts cuts, almost completely rejects color, and mixes the sophistication of Western couture with Japanese sobriety. Contrasts of black and white lend sharpness to his linear designs, often inspired by men's fashions. He envelops the body rather than emphasizing it, resulting in an unconventional but nonetheless poetic and well-proportioned fashion that quite simply lies beyond trends. And for which there is only one appropriate term: avant-garde.

That in a mere two years the initial aversion to his creations was transformed into pure admiration speaks to the power and originality of his ideas. And it is proof that a change had already taken place in people's minds. His

fashion became the status symbol of creative urbanites. In 1987, the current fashion star Azzedine Alaïa (see page 80) left his studio in the middle of preparations for his own show to see the presentation by his Japanese colleague.

Yamamoto, who not only has a preference for black, but also has a black belt in karate, had never expected success. His aim, he once confessed, had been to design clothing in peace and quiet. But before he could fulfill this dream, he first had to study law. His mother, who raised him on her own after the death of his father in the war, earning a living as a seamstress, insisted on it. Yamamoto obeyed, but immediately exchanged his law books for pattern books, and in 1969, at the age of twenty-six, graduated from the renowned Bunka Fashion College. In 1972 he founded his label Y's Inc., fiddled around with pattern cutting in the back room of his mother's store, and five years later presented his first collection in Tokyo. A tremendous success, the well-known local Seibu store set up a special corner for his wide, tent-like garments. Together with his girlfriend at the time, the designer Rei Kawakubo (see page 90), he went to Paris. They were among the first foreign designers whose names appeared in the official prêt-à-porter calendar. Today, Yamamoto's name appears on the door of flagship stores all over the world.

1943 Born in Yokohama, Japan,
on October 3
1966 Completes law studies at Keio
University in Tokyo
1966–69 Studies fashion at the Bunka
Fukuso Gakuin in Tokyo
1972 Launch of his first personal label,
Y's
1977 Presents his first collection in
Tokyo
1981 First presentation of his collections at the Paris fashion shows
1985 Opens his first flagship store in
Tokyo
1995 Costume design for Daniel
Barenboim's production of
Richard Wagner's opera *Tristan
and Isolde* in Bayreuth
SINCE 2003 Creation of the upscale
product line Y-3 for Adidas

left
Ensemble from the spring/summer 2010
prêt-à-porter collection

above
Yohji Yamamoto, 2009

JIL SANDER

ROMY SCHNEIDER

WIM WENDERS

1903 First Tour de France

1938 Kristallnacht in Nazi German

1886 Statue of Liberty erected in
New York Harbor

1913–27 Marcel Proust publishes
A la recherche du temps perdu

1950–53 Korean War

1929 First television images broadcast

1880　1885　1890　1895　1900　1905　1910　1915　1920　1925　1930　1935　1940　1945　1950　1955　1960　1965

Summer 1992 collection

Summer 1994 collection

4 Civil rights legislation to end racial
segregation in the U.S.

1994 End of apartheid in South Africa

2001 First same-sex marriage
in the Netherlands

1977 First *Star Wars* film directed by George Lucas

| 1970 | 1975 | 1980 | 1985 | 1990 | 1995 | 2000 | 2005 | 2010 | 2015 | 2020 | 2025 | 2030 | 2035 | 2040 | 2045 | 2050 | 2055 |

JIL SANDER

A master of understatement, she put Germany on the fashion map. Her self-confident minimalism earned her the title the "Queen of Less."

To be successful in fashion, it is important to have a clear vision. And Heidemarie Jiline Sander's vision has deep roots: in the early fifties the seven-year-old was made to wear skirts puffed out with petticoats like her classmates. The girl preferred pants. So it is no surprise that twenty years later that same girl boldly set out to revolutionize women's fashion.

In the late sixties, Sander, an experienced textile engineer, opened a boutique in Pöseldorf, an upscale district of Hamburg. Her first step toward realizing her vision was to get rid of her first name. ("I couldn't call my business 'Heidi Sander,' that sounds so German, so sweet.") In her battle against excess and ostentation, the cool blonde German at first sold exclusively boutique fashion ordered from Paris. In 1973 she released her first collection: unadorned linear pieces, guaranteed to be cliché-free. Instinctively, Sander was already committing herself to the style that would later bring international fame—but with her uncompromising minimalism she was too far ahead of her contemporaries. Her debut at Paris Fashion Week in 1975 was savaged or, almost worse, ignored by the press. Why? Next to the opulent creations of the Parisian couturiers, her sleek minimalist pieces borrowing the fabric and cut of men's fashion were mercilessly overlooked. But she was not to be deterred. She moved to Milan, where quality craftsmanship was more appreciated, and stayed loyal to her style until justified by success.

In the mid-eighties Sander's ideas began to meet with demand. Women were increasingly taking on managerial roles in business, and her perfectly cut pantsuits ("No quality without form!") in neutral colors, combined with white dress shirts and slender trench coats, soon became their global uniform. The idea that simplicity can also mean luxury took hold.

With her first international success, Jil Sander realized that in order to make it last she had to position her brand worldwide. Even before globalization and industrialization reached the fashion industry, her label was one of the first fashion enterprises listed on a stock exchange. The money she made was promptly invested in gigantic flagship stores in Tokyo and New York, monumental works of architecture whose construction swallowed up millions. Now, if not before, it was clear to all: Jil Sander was at the peak of her success.

The problems began in 1999, when Sander sold the majority of her shares to the Prada Group. She could not come to terms with the new company strategy. It is said that she feared a decline in quality, and when asked to adapt her slender silhouettes to average sizes at odds with her exacting proportions, she parted ways with the Italian luxury group. In 2003 she briefly returned as head designer, but a year later she finally made a clean break. For six years the media-shy fashion creator kept a low profile. Then, in 2009, came an unexpected comeback. As the new creative director of the Japanese fashion chain Uniqlo, her present aim is "to incorporate first-class quality in a brand with democratic prices"—quite in the spirit of her vision.

The Jil Sander label, today owned by the Japanese clothing company and its European subsidiary GIBO, continues at the height of fashion under creative director Raf Simons. Appointed in 2005, the Belgian with an industrial design background captures the spirit of the purist tradition in his collections through his strong tailoring and striking silhouettes, employing high-quality, innovative materials and the highest craftsmanship.

1943 Born in Wesselburen, Germany, on November 27
1968 Opens a fashion boutique in Hamburg
1973 Presents her first collection
1978 Founds her fashion house
1979 Launch of first perfume for women, Woman Pure, and for men, Man Pure
1993 Opens first flagship store in Paris
1994 Opens first showroom in Milan
2005 Raf Simons becomes chief designer at Jil Sander
2009 Comeback as new creative director of the Japanese fashion chain Uniqlo

Jil Sander, 2004

1903–40 Construction of the Baghdad Railway

1937 Pablo Picasso paints *Guernica*

1917 October Revolution in Russia

1946–54 Indochina War

1962 Cuban Missile Crisis

1891 The company Philips is founded in the Netherlands

1928 Alexander Fleming discovers penicillin

1880　1885　1890　1895　1900　1905　1910　1915　1920　1925　1930　1935　1940　1945　1950　1955　1960　1965

Linda Evangelista, Cindy Crawford,
Naomi Campbell, and Christy Turlington
show creations from the fall/winter
1991/92 collection

1972 Hostage crisis at the Munich
Summer Olympics

2000–5 Second Palestinian Intifada

1988 The exhibition *Freeze* in London leads to the
breakthrough of the Young British Artists

| 1970 | 1975 | 1980 | 1985 | 1990 | 1995 | 2000 | 2005 | 2010 | 2015 | 2020 | 2025 | 2030 | 2035 | 2040 | 2045 | 2050 | 2055 |

GIANNI VERSACE

The opulent creations of the Italian designer are emblematic of the glamour, sexuality, and swagger of the 1980s.

"Maximalist," "Master of neo-Baroque," "Sun king." When it was a question of finding a suitable title for Gianni Versace, the press was rarely stingy with the superlatives. And there was no need to be, for no one abhorred understatement more than the Italian designer himself. "Less is not more," he liked to remark, "Less is less." And it was the same with his fashion.

As far as his opulent creations were concerned, Gianni Versace knew absolutely no taboos. His knowledge of art history was said to be impressive, but did not hinder him in the least from combining the most opposed artistic styles, bold colors (above all purple, red, and yellow), and patterns from diverse cultures with an uninhibited extravagance, sometimes to the very limits of the tolerable. Versace's blunt comment was: "Good taste does not interest me. For me there is no 'too much.'" Even with his ever-lavish working of materials, Versace loved opulence and the deliberate use of contrasts. Solid denim was combined with delicate lace, crêpe de Chine with heavy studs, and cool nappa leather with velvet embroidered with glass beads. The fabric he developed, called Oroton, consisted entirely of metal, yet could be worked like the softest and smoothest textiles. His garments adorned with the head of Medusa (Versace's trade-mark and part of the company logo) were a symbol of ecstasy, glamour, and excess. And a good helping of sex. For some even too much, as so often the case with Versace. "Why not look daring sometimes? Why not sexy? Why not vulgar? Convention can be cracked like an oyster," said the designer in a self-confident challenge to his critics. And indeed Versace had little use for convention. Where clothes were concerned, he treated women and men alike in an almost pedantic fashion. His wildly patterned, gold-buttoned silk shirts for men were no less eye-catching than his women's models.

Versace was born in 1946 in Calabria, at the extreme tip of the boot that forms the map of Italy. His mother was a dressmaker to the prominent families of the province, his father a salesman. In the early seventies, after breaking off his study of architecture, he left the deep south in order to work as a designer in Milan. In 1978 he presented fashion for the first time under his own name, giving Italian

1946 Born in Reggio Calabria, Italy,
on December 2
1964 Learns couture in his mother's
studio
1968–78 Independent fashion designer
for various Italian manufacturers
1978 Founds the Gianni Versace label
and presents his first collections
for women and men
1979 Opens his first boutique in Milan
1981 Launch of his first perfume,
Donna
FROM 1989 Introduces the secondary
line for young people, Versus; and
in the U.S. the V2 By Versace line,
the classic Signature line, and the
Home Signature furnishing line
1997 Shot in Miami Beach on July 15;
sister Donatella Versace carries
on the label

left
Naomi Campbell presents a creation
from the summer 1991 collection

above
Gianni Versace
Donatella Versace

fashion a facet then unknown. With his conspicuous style, Versace soon developed into the antithesis of Giorgio Armani (see page 60), who was by then already well established. "His thinking is as beige as his jackets. He comes from the north; I come from the south. We have absolutely nothing to say to each other," Versace liked to say about his rival.

His hard-earned wealth enabled Versace to lead a life that fit with his fashions: extravagant, ostentatious, spendthrift. On the morning of July 15, 1997, Gianni Versace was shot when leaving his Miami Beach villa. Shock was followed by a great surprise: the couturier had made his favorite niece Allegra his principal heir, as a result of which she has become the most influential woman in Italian fashion. The creative legacy of the house was inherited by Versace's muse and sister Donatella, who at first seemed to suffer in this new and unexpected role. In Donatella's hands, Gianni's complex opulence turned into crudely flamboyant sexuality. Over the years, however, the self-styled "Versace girl" has learned to interpret her brother's heritage in a contemporary way, even to step out of his shadow. The press celebrates her latest collections as a modern version of the Versace style. Donatella has said, "My brother was a genius. I am not. But Gianni was the best teacher I could have had."

left
Gianni Versace spring/summer 2010
collection

right page
Gianni Versace fall/winter 2008/09
collection

1892 Premiere of the ballet *The Nutcracker*
by Peter Tchaikovsky at the Mariinsky
Theater in St. Petersburg

1909 First seagoing vessel with diesel engine

1921 Ireland wins independence
from the United Kingdom

1933 Diego Rivera paints
Man at the Crossroads

1947 Otto Frank
publishes
*The Diary of
Anne Frank*

1957 Launch of the first
artificial earth
satellite, *Sputnik*,
by the Soviet Union

| 1880 | 1885 | 1890 | 1895 | 1900 | 1905 | 1910 | 1915 | 1920 | 1925 | 1930 | 1935 | 1940 | 1945 | 1950 | 1955 | 1960 | 1965 |

FURSTENBERG

A wrap dress from the spring/summer 2006
prêt-à-porter collection

1973 Yom Kippur War

1989 The portable game console
Game Boy goes on sale

2007–9 Global financial crisis

2002 U.S. detention camp set up
at Guantánamo

| 1970 | 1975 | 1980 | 1985 | 1990 | 1995 | 2000 | 2005 | 2010 | 2015 | 2020 | 2025 | 2030 | 2035 | 2040 | 2045 | 2050 | 2055 |

DIANE VON FURSTENBERG

In the 1970s, her invention the wrap dress became a symbol of liberation, success, and glamour. It was rediscovered in the nineties.

"Feel like a woman, wear a dress!" A simple statement, a simple idea, a magnificent success. In 1974 Diane von Furstenberg created a dress that was not only to change her life, but also that of millions of other women: the wrap dress. Uncomplicated to wear, both elegant and sexy, it liberated the "working woman" from the androgynous pants suit. In 1976, having sold several millions of her wrap dresses within a remarkably short time, the designer appeared on the cover of the *Newsweek* as an icon of women's liberation and the most profitable fashion designer since Coco Chanel (see page 20). At the time, Diane von Furstenberg was not yet thirty years old.

The image of the high-powered American woman, one who tirelessly pursues a career but also knows how to have a good time, not only inspired the collections of Diane von Furstenberg, it was also shaped by her. Born Diane Halfin in Belgium, she moved to New York in 1969 with her new husband. He was a successful Wall Street banker with an aristocratic pedigree, she a young, beautiful woman with style; and both quickly gained a foothold in New York's high society. But rather than leading a glamorous life at her husband's side, as was then the custom, Diane von Furstenberg began her career as a designer following the birth of her second child. And a short time later, she was divorced. Only two years after her start as a designer and her first fashion shows (for which she had to hire models from a fashion school), she developed her masterpiece, the wrap dress. The first cotton jersey wrap dresses sold for ninety dollars; they were manufactured in Italy to Diane von Furstenberg's specifications and stamped with zebra prints, waves, and other designs. In quick succession there followed dress models in silk jersey, a luggage line, eyeglasses, and cosmetics.
The strength of her masterpiece not only lies in its being suitable for every occasion and for women

of all ages and figures. It is characterized by an additional quality not typically associated with trendy looks: it is timeless. This is the only explanation for the fact that in the nineties Diane von Furstenberg experienced something that rarely happens to any designer during their lifetime: her own comeback. After her success had faded away in the eighties as quickly as it had begun, a whole new generation of women suddenly discovered, in flea markets and vintage boutiques, these flowing, comfortable wrap dresses with their colorful patterns. The designer, who had meanwhile retired from fashion and founded a publishing house in Paris, returned to New York.
In 1997 she celebrated the comeback of her wrap dress, and five years later her company was operating in the black. Diane von Furstenberg hasn't grown tired of her fashion classic yet. Each of her unfailingly glamorous collections includes at least one wrap dress.

1946 Born in Brussels on December 31
FROM 1964 Studies Spanish in Madrid and business management in Geneva
1970 First women's fashion designs
1972 Founds her own fashion label
1975 Launch of the perfume Tatiana
1985 Founds the French-language publishing house Salvy in Paris
1991 Enters the home shopping business
1997 Re-launch of her fashion label and start of a new career as fashion designer
1998 Publishes her memoirs under the title *Diane: A Signature Life*
2003 Designs the tennis collection RBK by DVF together with Venus Williams and Reebok

Diane von Furstenberg, 2009

1890 First execution via the electric chair of a prisoner sentenced to death

1919 Founding of the Bauhaus in Weimar, Germany

1936 Guido Fanconi identifies the metabolic disorder cystic fibrosis

1961 Construct of the Be Wall

1905 Russian Revolution

1949 Indonesia wins independence from the Netherlands

1880 1885 1890 1895 1900 1905 1910 1915 1920 1925 1930 1935 1940 1945 1950 1955 1960 1965

Semitransparent body with stand-up collar and matching stole from the fall/winter 1998/99 haute couture collection

1976 First G7 summit   **1995** Sweden, Finland, and Austria join the EU

1985 Mikhail Gorbachev becomes general
secretary of the Communist Party
of the Soviet Union   **2006** Montenegro declares independence
from Serbia

1970   1975   1980   1985   1990   1995   2000   2005   2010   2015   2020   2025   2030   2035   2040   2045   2050   2055

THIERRY MUGLER

Mugler created a kind of "superwoman," sexy and self-confident, with wide shoulders and a narrow wasp waist.

He thoroughly deserved his nickname "Créateur de Choc" (creator of shock). In his fashion career of almost thirty years, everything Thierry Mugler did was out of the ordinary. He replaced the carefree folksy woman of the seventies with a seductress in a razor-sharp silhouette. He designed couture clothes in latex and metal. He not only presented his creations to a select circle of insiders, but also staged large, public fashion spectacles. And he never concerned himself with trends, but consistently promoted his stylized superwoman with strong shoulders and a wasp waist, whom he at times covered with a leather carapace, butterfly wings, or a robot suit. Mugler seemed to have come from another planet, but his unmistakable style that defined the eighties and nineties continues to inspire designers today. "I did make clothes because I was looking for something that didn't exist," Mugler said, looking back. "I have to try to create my own world."

That Strasbourg, France, his hometown, was not the right place for a fashion fantasist like him soon became clear. As a youth, Mugler was already drawing attention with his self-designed clothes. An inattentive student but a disciplined dancer, as a teenager he was a member of a ballet company. He was to take two things with him when he left the city at the age of twenty: his enthusiasm for stage productions and his love of perfect bodies, expressed in each of his heroic creations that idealized the human anatomy. After first working in Paris in a boutique and as a fashion illustrator and window dresser, in 1973 he struck out on his own and at age twenty-five presented his first independent collection, Café de Paris. The press was thrilled about his femme fatale—self-confident in sharply cut black suits and trench coats—that banished the then-ubiquitous flower child.
The Mugler fashion house attracted attention for far more than its racy style. It was also among the few labels with their own factory. And Mugler designed everything himself—from dresses to advertisements (an avid photographer, he often took the pictures himself), to the futuristic boutiques and his fashion shows that quickly became major events choreographed like Broadway musicals. To commemorate the tenth anniversary of the brand, he invited a paying audience of 6,000 to a superlative fashion show. He marked his twentieth anniversary with a spectacle transmitted live on television, costing 18 million francs and featuring 120 models. Though he never had formal training in tailoring, beginning in 1992 Mugler presented an official haute couture collection. Today he basks in more than his reputation as the brilliant fantasist who dreamed up "Catwoman outfits" in black vinyl. Another of his classic creations was a supremely elegant suit with a skintight pencil skirt, tightly waisted jacket, emphasized shoulders, and protruding peplum. And his evening gowns radiate the glamour of old Hollywood—even when made of rubber lace.
But fashion alone has never been enough for the multitalented Mugler. In 2000 he retired from his label to dedicate his time to the production of stage shows, photography, and film. A collection bearing his name still exists, but he does not design it.

1948 Born in Strasbourg on December 21
1962–64 Trains as a ballet dancer and studies at the École des Arts Décoratifs in Strasbourg
1973 Presents his first collection under the brand name Café de Paris
1974 Founds his own label
1978 Opens his first boutique in Paris
1979 Introduces a men's line
1983 Opens his own factory
1992 First haute couture collection and launch of his first perfume, Angel
1997 The company Clarins acquires shares in the label
2001 Retires from the fashion business and concentrates on the creation of perfumes and photography

Thierry Mugler, 2003

1903 The Wright brothers, Wilbur and Orville, make the first engine-powered flight

1932 Founding of the Kingdom of Saudi Arabia

1954 Premiere of Alfred Hitchcock's *Rear Window*

1888 Founding of the National Geographic Society for the promotion of geography

1919 Germany's colonies in Africa taken over by the U.K. and France

1942 Edward Hopper paints *Nighthawks*

1880 1885 1890 1895 1900 1905 1910 1915 1920 1925 1930 1935 1940 1945 1950 1955 1960 1965

DONNA KARAN
NEW YORK

Aborigines in Australia
granted full civil rights

1995 Launch of the Japanese electronic
toy Tamagotchi

1982 Michael Jackson releases
the album *Thriller*

2004 Eastern expansion of the EU

| 1970 | 1975 | 1980 | 1985 | 1990 | 1995 | 2000 | 2005 | 2010 | 2015 | 2020 | 2025 | 2030 | 2035 | 2040 | 2045 | 2050 | 2055 |

DONNA KARAN

This New York designer is famous for comfortable chic and functional power dressing.

The greatest successes are usually based on simple ideas. In the case of Donna Karan there were precisely seven: seven black, functional items of clothing, all of which could be combined with any other. These "Seven Easy Pieces"—bodysuit, blouse, skirt, pants, jacket, coat, and a simple evening dress—comprised the New York designer's first independent collection. And it was an immediate, overwhelming success.

Over the years Donna Karan has built up an empire, but her principles have remained unchanged. This designer does not consider herself a couturier, but a woman who solves other women's clothing problems. Her collections are still grounded in the principle that all articles of clothing must, regardless of seasonal trends, be interchangeable and combinable with each other. They are made for people "who never know where the day is going to take them"—that is, for people like Donna Karan herself. The New Yorker's straightforward creations are so authentic (and successful) because they embody the prototype of her own target group: women who have mastered the delicate balancing act between career and family, who are wives and business-women in equal measure—and who do not necessarily have a perfect figure. Karan's designs are intended to favorably accentuate the wearer's figure while at the same time conceal what should not be seen. After all, the designer, who herself wears a size 10, is convinced that every woman "would like to look slimmer, taller, more beautiful, without any great effort."

Donna Karan was born in 1948 in the city responsible for her "tempo and mindset" and that continues to inspire her: New York. As the daughter of a tailor and a model, fashion is literally in her genes. She studied fashion at New York's renowned Parsons School of Design, but after a summer internship with the designer Anne Klein, the nineteen-year-old Karan never returned to class. Seven years later,

after the early death of Anne Klein, together with Louis Dell'Olio she took over the management of the company. Her only daughter (who was later to inspire her to create her younger, more profitable spin-off line, DKNY) had been born only a week earlier. With her second husband, the sculptor Stephan Weiss, and the financial support of a Japanese enterprise, she finally founded her own label in 1984. After twelve high-flying years, she went public—and got an unpleasant surprise. The designer, until then spoiled by success, found herself in the red. Her solution was to concentrate on her strength, design, and to hand over the running of her business to others. It was a smart move. In 2001 she sold the company for $643 million to the luxury firm LVMH. As chief creative director, however, she still ensures that her name sells nothing other than her philosophy: high-quality, well-cut fashion for women who in fact have no time for fashion.

1948 Born in New York on October 2
FROM 1966 Studies at Parsons School
of Design in New York
1968–74 Design assistant, later
associate designer at Anne Klein
1974–84 Chief designer at the house
of Anne Klein together with
Louis Dell'Olio after the death
of Anne Klein
1984 Founds her own business with
husband Stephan Weiss
1985 Presents her first collection
1988 Launches the lower-priced DKNY
line
1992 Introduces a men's line
1992 Launches her first perfume,
Donna Karan New York
1994 Opens her first flagship store
in London
2001 The business is taken over by
the luxury organization LVMH
2002 Gives up the creative direction
of the fashion house

left page
Donna Karan campaign

above
Donna Karan, 2009

MIUCCIA PRADA ▬▬▬▬▬▬▬▬

MADELEINE ALBRIGHT ▬▬▬▬▬▬▬▬▬▬▬▬▬▬▬▬▬

CINDY SHERMAN ▬▬▬▬▬▬▬

1910–29 Mexican Revolution   **1935** Founding of Alcoholics Anonymous   **1961** Founding
                                                                                                    Amnesty
1898 Pierre and Marie Curie   **1925** F. Scott Fitzgerald publishes   **1945** U.S. atomic bomb attacks on   Internatio
discover radium   *The Great Gatsby*   Hiroshima and Nagasaki

1880   1885   1890   1895   1900   1905   1910   1915   1920   1925   1930   1935   1940   1945   1950   1955   1960   1965

Prada advertising campaign
spring/summer, 2005

1975 Beginning of the Pol Pot
regime in Cambodia

1998 Marketing of the medication Sildenafil,
known by the brand name Viagra

1989 George H. W. Bush becomes
41st U.S. president

2006 A special Iraqi tribunal sentences
Saddam Hussein to death

| 1970 | 1975 | 1980 | 1985 | 1990 | 1995 | 2000 | 2005 | 2010 | 2015 | 2020 | 2025 | 2030 | 2035 | 2040 | 2045 | 2050 | 2055 |

MIUCCIA PRADA

This Milanese designer successfully combines art and commerce in her creations. Since the early 1990s, she and her labels Prada and Miu Miu have enjoyed absolute cult status on the fashion scene.

Of all things, it was a nylon backpack. Feather-light, functional, and without frills, it appeared in the middle of the logo-laden eighties, and didn't quite seem to fit with the flashy zeitgeist. And even less with the image of a label that had been producing fine leather goods since 1913: Prada. But this first stroke of genius alone demonstrates the unique talent of its creator. With this black nylon backpack, Miuccia Prada was not just creating a trend; she was laying the cornerstone for a trend empire with several fashion and accessory lines, flagship stores all over the world, a cosmetic line, and an art foundation of its own. Ultimately Prada has achieved a cult status that, rather than flicker out, reignites with every season. From neat school-uniform styles to a rumpled-linen look, from baby-doll dresses with harlequin motifs to coats in upholstery fabrics and evening gowns decorated with zippers—Miuccia Prada has an endless source of creativity at her command.

The absurd part of it is that this Italian woman who sets trends with each new season had no design experience at all when, in 1978, she joined her grandfather's business. She had a degree in political science, studied acting, and a weakness for Communism. This may not sound like ideal casting, but she turned out to be the best choice imaginable for the role. Simply because Miuccia Prada was so different, the Prada label was also to become strikingly different. That backpack, produced as early as 1985 in a style that would not became known until the nineties as minimalism, was only a small taste of what to expect from Signora Prada. Four years later, her first fashion collection hit the market. "Uniforms for the slightly disenfranchised" was the title of this first, serious collection. Such concepts quickly explain why Miuccia Prada enjoys a reputation as an intellectual among fashion designers. The Milanese designer's progressive style driving her to experiment with prints and fabrics from handmade lace to teddy-bear mohair, to shift proportions, to combine lime green with kidney brown, and to continually question and advance modern ideas of aesthetics, is often described as "anti-chic" chic. Miuccia Prada cannot be pigeon-holed, if only because, by her own account, she finds it particularly stimulating to contradict herself from one season to the next. Cool minimalism, functional "Utilitarian Chic," consciously bourgeois "Geek Chic," the nostalgic "vintage look"—a small

1949 Born in Milan on May 10
BEFORE 1978 Drama training with Giorgio Strehler at the Piccolo Teatro in Milan; graduates with a PhD in political science
1978 Assumes the management of Prada, founded by her grand-father
1983 Presents her first shoe collection
1985 Presents her first women's prêt-à-porter collection
1992 Introduces the lower-priced Miu Miu line and a men's line
1995 Founding of the Fondazione Prada for the promotion of up-and-coming talent
1998 Introduces the Prada Sportswear label
1999 Takes over the fashion houses of Jil Sander and Helmut Lang (until their resale in 2006)

left
Dresses in graphic pattern from the Miu Miu spring/summer 2005 collection

above
Miuccia Prada, 1999

selection from the great trends of the last twenty years in which she played an integral part.

"I hate fashion," Miuccia Prada once said, "I also love it, of course…. The way we think of ourselves, the way we compose ourselves every day, for me this is very profound." The long lines at her fashion shows and her multibillion-dollar income are the proof of just how many people trust her to dress them.

Presentation of the Prada fall/winter 2009/10 prêt-à-porter collection

1903 Founding of the Kraft Foods
company

1936 Premiere of Charlie Chaplin's
film *Modern Times*

1890 First vaccination of a human
with immune serum

1920–30 Harlem Renaissance

1953 Decoding of the structure
of deoxyribonucleic acid
(DNA)

1880 1885 1890 1895 1900 1905 1910 1915 1920 1925 1930 1935 1940 1945 1950 1955 1960 1965

Art. Moschino   SIRONI/GC&P

STOP THE FASHION SYSTEM !

MOSCHINO

above
"Mickey Mouse," fall/winter
1987/88, by Franco Moschino

right
Franco Moschino, drawing for
"Stop the Fashion System!"

Assassination of John F. Kennedy

1991 Collapse of the USSR

2007 The Apple iPhone goes
on sale

1978 Forming of the band
Dire Straits

2000 The dot-com bubble bursts

| 1970 | 1975 | 1980 | 1985 | 1990 | 1995 | 2000 | 2005 | 2010 | 2015 | 2020 | 2025 | 2030 | 2035 | 2040 | 2045 | 2050 | 2055 |

FRANCO MOSCHINO

"Classico con twist" was the motto of the designer who made fashion fun.

Franco Moschino had a short career: ten years. But these ten years were enough for him to develop a truly unique reputation in the world of fashion: he was the anti-designer with a twinkle in his eye. His brand attracted attention not so much through its clothes (which tended to be classic), but through their wit and message. Moschino understood fashion as a medium. So he used it to show the industry, which had gained enormous influence in the label-obsessed eighties, its own limits. He held a mirror up to consumer society, writing "For Fashion Victims Only" on a shirt with overlong sleeves crossing the body like a straitjacket, and adorned a Chanel-style suit with the phrase "This is a Waste of Money." His disrespectful sense of humor and his surrealist ideas—decorating a dinner jacket with real cutlery, and dresses with teddy-bear collars—earned him the status of an outsider among the Milan fashion czars Armani (see page 60), Ferré, and Versace (see page 96). But this did not bother Franco Moschino. "I am not a designer," he proclaimed, and went as far as demanding the end of fashion in a 1991 campaign. But what sounds counterproductive became a fabulous success, and the self-appointed "philosopher of fashion" became an important figure in an industry on which he had originally declared war.

The designer who did not want to be a designer and yet was one actually began as an art student and saw himself as an artist. Born in 1950 in Italy, Moschino experienced to the fullest the early eighties of logo mania, ostentatious luxury, and the belief that clothes really do make the man. After his studies at the Milan Academy of Fine Arts, he actually worked for a number of years as a fashion illustrator for the glamour designer Gianni Versace. He came to the conclusion that clothes were more important than the world of fashion, and that they should be fun. It was with this mission that he founded his label in 1983.

For some, Moschino, who quite openly admitted copying from colleagues, was a pioneer of fashion, for others a *mantenuto*, a "kept man." He did not invent anything new; he only interpreted it in a new way. A cocktail dress crowned by a military aircraft for a hat, a skirt made of men's neckties, and slogans such as "Expensive Jacket" on a cashmere jacket are just a few examples of his fashion parodies.

In 1991 Moschino took a radical decision—not to put on any more catwalk shows, and to begin his legendary "Stop the Fashion System" advertising campaign. But this didn't stop his fans either. Rather than attending his fashion shows, the press instead beat a path to his showroom. Moschino celebrated his ten-year anniversary—incidentally also his farewell—in 1993 with a big retrospective at the Milan National Theater. He died the following year. His successor was his closest and longest-standing assistant, Rossella Jardini. The Moschino motto "Classico con Twist" (classic with a twist) has since then been successfully brought by Jardini from the revolutionary phase into adulthood. She refrains from criticizing the fashion system, preferring to play with charmingly interpreted classics and the hearts and ribbons characteristic of the brand. The old irony is found above all in the surrealist-inspired design of window displays and boutiques, in which sofas are shaped like oversize moneybags and lamps grow out of boots. It is only recently that Jardini has begun to appear in person on the catwalk at the end of fashion shows. For thirteen years she declined to do so, out of respect for Franco Moschino.

1950 Born in Abbiategrasso, Italy, on February 27
1968–71 Studies at the Academy of Arts in Milan
1970–80 Illustrator for fashion magazines and freelance designer for various Italian fashion firms
1983 Founds his own business and presents his first women's collection
1985 Presents his first men's collection
1987 Launches his first perfume, Moschino
1988 Introduces his Cheap and Chic line
1989 Opens the first Moschino boutique in Milan
1994 Dies in Milan on September 18

Franco Moschino

1891 Carnegie Hall opens in New York

1898 Spanish-American War

1911 Roald Amundsen becomes first to reach the geographic South Pole

1927 Premiere of the first talking picture, *The Jazz Singer*

1941 Japanese attack on Pearl Harbor

1958 Truman Capote publishes *Breakfast at Tiffany's*

1880 1885 1890 1895 1900 1905 1910 1915 1920 1925 1930 1935 1940 1945 1950 1955 1960 1965

A model shows a taffeta bolero with ruffled collar and sleeves over a calf-length green skirt from the fall/winter 1991/92 haute couture collection

CHRISTIAN LACROIX

He turned haute couture upside down with his opulent creations, and was the embodiment of the extravagant 1980s.

"Dresses must be costumes." A piece of advice on life from his grandfather. About twenty years later, it was to be the key to a unique career in fashion. Christian Lacroix did not debut on the catwalk with a ready-to-wear collection but went straight into haute couture, and took eighties fashion in an entirely new direction. With his extravagantly staged shows he transformed the presentation of fashion into a gesamtkunstwerk. And with his unconventional mixtures of styles and patterns, he showed fans of "power dressing" the power of imagination.

For a long time, Christian Lacroix was completely unaware of this power, and of his own talent. The future "king of fashion who came out of nowhere" had never intended to stand in the limelight or become the embodiment of the extravagant fashion of the late eighties. His profession of choice was museum curator. Born and bred in the 2,000-year-old southern French city of Arles, from the Roman and Romanesque monuments to the historic bull-fighting arena he found a fertile breeding ground for his great passion—history, particularly the history of costume. For hours at a time he rummaged among his grandmother's back issues of *La Mode Illustrée*, copying and modifying what he saw. A design career seemed imminent. But after leaving school with the firm intention of one day organizing museum exhibitions, he studied French literature, and in 1971 moved to Paris to write a thesis on costume in seventeenth-century painting. But instead of gaining access to the capital's highly competitive museum world, the door to the fashion world opened to him when he met his future wife. While working for a PR and marketing agency, Françoise Rosensthiel was convinced of Lacroix's talent and introduced him to her boss. When the latter moved to Jean Patou's haute couture house, he took Lacroix with him—as his designer. In his collections for Patou it became clear that Christian

Lacroix was different. The Paris fashion scene was celebrating the minimalist-conceptual ready-to-wear fashion of Yohji Yamamoto (see page 92) and Comme des Garçons when a colorful ball destroyed the fine, well-thought-out black order: the "pouf," an extremely bouffant, tantalizing balloon skirt soon to be copied by everyone. With the founding of his own fashion house and his first haute couture show in 1987, Christian Lacroix became an overnight star.

The American department stores Bloomingdale's and Bergdorf Goodman battled for the privilege to be the first to show his clothes. Bloomingdale's won: "Outfit Number 27," a cocktail dress in brown, pink and yellow, appeared in their Lexington Avenue window. Sale price: $15,000.

"I am a virtuoso at recycling on a dizzying journey through the fashion of the last three centuries," said Christian Lacroix about himself. There is no better description of his opulent style. Crinoline skirts, torero jackets, stripes, checks, lace, tweed, brocade, and shimmering silks—everything found its place under his hands. The late eighties was the right time for a fantasist like Lacroix. Women tired of the career uniform look of their "power suits" desired a return to a fashion that was feminine and fun. Christian Lacroix gave them both, wrapped up in a dynamic catwalk show.

With breathtaking clothes that earned him the reputation of being one of the last tailors who still made genuine haute couture, the euphoria over the house of Christian Lacroix lasted into the nineties. And the Italian Pucci label, famous for its colorful prints, also benefited for a time from his virtuosity. Yet in May 2009 the house had to declare itself insolvent. Not once in twenty-two years had it turned a profit.

1951 Born in Arles, France, on May 16
1969 Studies French literature in Montpellier
1971 Moves to Paris and completes his studies with a dissertation on "Costumes in 17th-century Painting"
1973 Training as museum curator at the École du Louvre
1981–87 Chief designer at Jean Patou
1987 Founds his own couture house and presents his first haute couture collection
1988 Presents his first prêt-à-porter collection
1989 Launches accessories line and the perfume C'est La Vie
2009 Insolvency of the fashion house

Christian Lacroix, 2002

1909 Founding of Tel Aviv

1895–98 Cuban War of Independence

1924 First performance of George Gershwin's *Rhapsody in Blue*

1939 The German Wehrmacht marches into Poland on September 1

1954 The U.S. Supreme Court prohibits racial segregatic in public schools

| 1880 | 1885 | 1890 | 1895 | 1900 | 1905 | 1910 | 1915 | 1920 | 1925 | 1930 | 1935 | 1940 | 1945 | 1950 | 1955 | 1960 | 1965 |

Richly embroidered corsage from the spring/ summer 2005 haute couture collection

The Roman Curia abolishes the *Index of Prohibited Books*, in vigor since 1559

1991 The World Wide Web made publicly available

1978 Forming of the band Duran Duran

2001 Terrorist attacks in the U.S. on September 11

2009 Barack Obama receives the Nobel Peace Prize

| 1970 | 1975 | 1980 | 1985 | 1990 | 1995 | 2000 | 2005 | 2010 | 2015 | 2020 | 2025 | 2030 | 2035 | 2040 | 2045 | 2050 | 2055 |

JEAN PAUL GAULTIER

The enfant terrible of the French fashion scene sent shockwaves through the 1980s with his skirts for men. In the nineties he was celebrated as the savior of haute couture.

Probably no designer has shattered as many taboos in the course of his career as Jean Paul Gaultier. He used underwear as outerwear, put men in women's clothes, and brought fetish clothing and camp clichés to the catwalk. But Jean Paul Gaultier is not only famous for making men and women wear identical clothes, or for Madonna's corset with conical cups. He is also an outstanding couturier who dusted off haute couture with his radical ideas and brought a younger audience to fashion shows.

Jean Paul Gaultier was already attracting attention at school in his Paris suburb. He made drawings of revue dancers, and abandoned his education at eighteen without graduating. His path led straight into the studio of the designer Pierre Cardin, to whom he had sent sketches and so impressed that he was offered a job. For six years Gaultier tried to get a foothold in various couture houses. But the rigid world of Parisian tailoring tradition was not made for such a rebel, and in 1976, at the age of just twenty-four, he struck out on his own.

It is no surprise that a young, nonconformist designer like Jean Paul Gaultier was not interested in cheerful flower power, but rather its opposite—punk.

His first designs were greeted with weary smiles. But then, in 1983, came his first coup: the corset dress, in which he integrated undergarments into evening fashion. Two years later, in a collection with the meaningful title "Une garde-robe pour deux" (One wardrobe for two), he marked yet another milestone in fashion history: the man's skirt. It was such a controversial garment that models refused to wear it on the catwalk. "For me, a woman is not identified by wearing skirts or nylon stockings," said the designer in retrospect, "These are outdated categories. Why shouldn't a man wear them too?" Provocation had acquired a new name: Gaultier. And it was one that everyone would get to know. The eighties were the decade of designers and their logos adorned everything from blazers to briefs. With the help of a young community of fans who felt he understood them, Jean Paul Gaultier rapidly became the rock star among designers. He gave women body stockings made of lace, and pantsuits from under which sexy lingerie peeked out. Men were given not only skirts, but also transparent blue and white striped shirts and tight patent-leather pants. He mixed East and West, classic and punk, masculine and feminine. But despite all the broken rules, one thing about Gaultier's fashion was always correct: the quality. The Paris school of couture had not passed him by without leaving its mark. And the man who had been sacked by his first teacher, Pierre Cardin, after only a year, returned to haute couture in 1997. But this time as a celebrated star and innovator who brought new life to a dusty industry. Then, in 2003, came the official accolade from Paris: the traditional French label Hermès, known for its luxury leather goods, appointed the enfant terrible with the peroxide-blond crew cut as its new head designer.

1952 Born in Arceuil, France, on April 24
1970 Fashion illustrator at Pierre Cardin
1971–74 Fashion illustrator at Jean Patou
1976 Presents his first collection
1978 Founds his own label
1978–81 Partnership with the Japanese textile manufacturer Kashiyama
1990 Costume design for Madonna's "Blonde Ambition" tour
1993 Launch of his first perfume, Jean Paul Gaultier
1997 Presents his first haute couture collection and designs futuristic costumes for Luc Besson's film *The Fifth Element*
SINCE 2003 Chief designer of the women's collection at Hermès

Jean Paul Gaultier, 2004

"LE MALE" par Jean Paul Gaultier

left
Jean Paul Gaultier
campaign

right
Evening gown in
Madonna style from
the spring/summer
2007 haute couture
collection

1907–8 Gustav Klimt paints *The Kiss*

1930 Mahatma Gandhi leads the Salt March in protest against the British salt monopoly

1959 Allan Kaprow organizes first Happening at the Reuben Gallery in New

1895 First public film screening in Berlin

1918–20 Worldwide influenza epidemic claims the lives of more than 20 million people

1947 India wins independence from the United Kingdom

| 1880 | 1885 | 1890 | 1895 | 1900 | 1905 | 1910 | 1915 | 1920 | 1925 | 1930 | 1935 | 1940 | 1945 | 1950 | 1955 | 1960 | 1965 |

Cream tunic in jersey over a polyester pullover and skirt, 1998

1970 Willy Brandt kneels in front of the memorial to the Jewish ghetto in Warsaw

1993 Bill Clinton becomes 42nd U.S. president

1981 First space shuttle flight (*Columbia*)

2003 Completion of mapping of the human genome

| 1970 | 1975 | 1980 | 1985 | 1990 | 1995 | 2000 | 2005 | 2010 | 2015 | 2020 | 2025 | 2030 | 2035 | 2040 | 2045 | 2050 | 2055 |

HELMUT LANG

His "minimal chic" was the foundation for the unpretentious style of the 1990s. Today the Austrian designer is still considered the "father of cool."

He was the cult designer at the close of the twentieth century. All of a sudden, intellectuals not only immersed themselves in academic theory, they also wanted to wear exceptional clothes. Creative types suddenly felt the need to wear a fashionable uniform, and in artistic circles fashion sense became an instant must. The responsibility for this lies with Helmut Lang and his creation, "minimal chic."

From the start, the Austrian designer appeared indifferent to rapidly changing trends. At the age of twenty-three, the self-taught couturier opened his first Vienna boutique, Bou Bou Lang, which soon became an insider's secret among the fashionable avant-garde. In 1984 there followed his first collection for women, an ultra-modern version of Austrian folklore, and two years later he showed his designs at an exhibition on Vienna in the Centre Pompidou in Paris. His fantastic success enabled him to show his clothing on the catwalk—and the Helmut Lang label was born.

Lang's cool, radical designs made a definitive break with overheated eighties fashions: instead of frills, the Austrian designer relied on straight-lined, lightweight fabrics, and form-fitting cuts (today his slender two- and three-button jackets remain men's fashion classics). Decorative details were abolished without substitution. His color palette, based mainly on contrasts between light and dark, was applied to plastic, transparent chiffon, and synthetic fabrics. Helmut Lang's fashion did not overload the individual with creative theatricality, but discreetly allowed the wearer's personality to dominate. His supporters celebrated his unaffected approach as a "new kind of honesty," although

critics categorized his emphasis on simplicity as well-calculated provocation.

As unpretentious as his fashion, was his manner of presenting it. Instead of grandiose runway shows with extravagant stage effects, the designer's modestly made-up models with simple ponytails walked down a zigzag catwalk carpet in an industrial setting. The Austrian designer, believed to be reserved in his private life, was rarely seen. In fact, known as the intellectuals' designer, he himself soon came to be considered a complicated intellectual, which certainly did no harm to his elevated position in the fashion world. In 1998, when Lang moved his base from Paris to New York, all the dates in the fashion calendar were changed out of consideration. Lang's reaction was to cancel his show outright and present his New York collection on the Internet, where it was accessible to all. In 2000, when he became the first non-American accepted to the exclusive circle of the Council of Fashion Designers of America (CFDA), he simply failed to show up.

Lang finally retired from the fashion business in 2005. He sold his shares in his firm to the Prada group, which had already bought part of the label in 1999. "It just became more and more a business, more image, more fake. Business means face creams and relatively horrible purses." Lang had reached a point at which there was nowhere further to go in fashion. Once, in 1998, he said that he would actually have preferred to become an artist, but that he had too much respect for art to do so. Ten years later, it seems he has arrived: he presented his first solo art exhibition in a gallery in Hanover, Germany.

1956 Born in Vienna on March 10
1979 Opens a boutique in Vienna and sells his own designs
1986 Founds his own fashion business
1987 First men's collection
1990 Introduces a shoe collection
1998 Moves from Vienna to New York
1999 Partial takeover of the business by the Prada organization
2004 Sale of the entire business to Prada
2005 Gives up creative direction of the fashion house
2006 Prada sells the Helmut Lang label to the Japanese fashion organization Link Theory Holdings

left
The "negligee look," spring/summer 1994

above
Helmut Lang

1887–89 Eiffel Tower constructed in Paris   **1915** Kazimir Malevich paints *Black Square* *on White Ground*   **1945** U.S. atomic bombing of Hiroshima and Nagasaki

1900 Boxer Rebellion in China

1929 World economic crisis following the U.S. stock market crash on October 25   **1959** China annexe Tibet

| 1880 | 1885 | 1890 | 1895 | 1900 | 1905 | 1910 | 1915 | 1920 | 1925 | 1930 | 1935 | 1940 | 1945 | 1950 | 1955 | 1960 | 1965 |

Look from the spring/summer 2008 collection

MARTIN MARGIELA

Bold words are not always necessary to make a revolutionary statement. In fact, in the case of Martin Margiela no words are needed at all. The Belgian fashion designer is the phantom of the fashion business. His influence, on the other hand, is quite visible.

He allows no photographs, gives no interviews, and remains backstage during his fashion shows. Martin Margiela does the unthinkable in the personality-driven world of fashion—he remains invisible, almost to the point of provocation. He rejects not only the glamour customary to fashion, but also and above all eschews the creation of image on which a fashion label's value is often based.

What is known about him can be told in a nutshell. He graduated from the Antwerp Academy of Fine Arts, became a member of the Antwerp Six (see also page 124), and took his first job as an assistant to Jean Paul Gaultier (see page 114). He next founded his own label, Maison Martin Margiela, and also spent a few years as chief designer at Hermès. And while the few stages of his design career are known, Martin Margiela is not a design personality in the true sense. By his own wishes, it is the creations rather than Margiela that stand in the spotlight. To be precise, the clothes are not strictly his, but of a faceless collaborative effort of the members of Maison Martin Margiela.

Anyone attempting to talk to Margiela about his fashion will receive, if lucky, a cryptic reply by fax, always in the first person plural, always signed "MMM." And whoever manages to peer behind the scenes of his studio will, of course, not meet the master himself, but a group of seemingly un-hierarchical staff members dressed in identical white work coats. The impression conveyed is that MMM is not staffed by creative people, but by laboratory technicians, nurses, and doctors. The question begs to be asked: Does Maison Martin Margiela design fashion in the convention sense, or do they rather research it, cultivate it, and breath new life into it?

This is the impression one receives. Margiela, a pioneer of Deconstructionism, takes clothes apart and puts them together again, often in a way that seems disharmonious in the conventional sense.

1957 Born in Genk, Belgium, on April 9

1977–79 Studies fashion at the Academy of Fine Arts in Antwerp

1984–87 Design assistant at Jean Paul Gaultier in Paris

1988 Founds the fashion house Martin Margiela (Neuf S.A.S.) in Paris with Jenny Meirens and presents his first collection

1994 On September 7, simultaneous presentation of fall/winter collection in Paris, Milan, New York, Tokyo, London, and Bonn

1997 First solo show at Boijmans van Beuningen Museum in Rotterdam

1998–2003 Artistic direction of women's collection at house of Hermès

2002 The Martin Margiela fashion house acquired by Diesel

2009 Martin Margiela leaves his label

Look from the spring/summer 2009 collection

With exposed shoulder pads, linings, and seams, unhemmed edges, and dangling threads, the origin and artifice of the production process are unmasked. Margiela seeks to do nothing less than expose the tricks of the fashion trade. He redesigns and recycles old objects for use in couture garments, or affixes a stripe (typically white) onto a used garment that reveals its past as it slowly peels away. Typical Margiela creations are anarchic in an almost infantile way—his handbags made from high-heeled shoes, sweaters of army socks, and tops sewn from leather gloves hover between trash and poetry. And one other thing is common to all Margiela pieces: their labeling and presentation.

Margiela remains true to his "incognito" strategy when presenting his collections. So as not to draw attention away from the collection, models remain anonymous behind stocking masks, long thick fringes, or plain black bars. Likewise, Margiela does not sign his creations. The Belgian designer places no value on the evidence of authenticity so important to designer fashions. A white laundry tag hand-sewn into the garment with four pick stitches serves as a label, which are left blank, or carry only a circled number. Ironically, this non-logo (the four stitches are visible from the outside and look to the uninitiated like a manufacturing defect) has for those in the know become a coveted trademark. The absence of a brand name paradoxically gives the label a striking visibility. Whether this was the intention of the creator remains unknown.

Anonymous models at the spring/summer
2009 prêt-à-porter collections

1907 Pablo Picasso paints
Les Demoiselles d'Avignon

1930 Marlene Dietrich begins her international
film career with *The Blue Angel*

1957 The Treaty of Rome
founds the Europea
Economic Commun
(EEC)

1893 First performance of Antonín Dvořák's
Ninth Symphony (*From the New World*)

1917 The U.S. enters
World War I

1944 Landing of the Allies
in Normandy

| 1880 | 1885 | 1890 | 1895 | 1900 | 1905 | 1910 | 1915 | 1920 | 1925 | 1930 | 1935 | 1940 | 1945 | 1950 | 1955 | 1960 | 1965 |

Look from the fall/winter 2008/09
collection

1973 Yom Kippur War

1986 Explosion of the space
shuttle *Challenger*

1998 Founding of the International
Criminal Court in The Hague

2007 Assassination of Pakistani
politician Benazir Bhutto

| | | | | | | | | | | | | | | | | | |
|1970|1975|1980|1985|1990|1995|2000|2005|2010|2015|2020|2025|2030|2035|2040|2045|2050|2055|

DRIES VAN NOTEN

In the 1980s, together with five Belgian colleagues he made Antwerp a center of avant-garde fashion. His designs, inspired by ethnic styles, exemplify timeless beauty.

"My aim is to create fashion that in a certain way is neutral—each person can let their personality flow into it." Dries Van Noten is considered one of the silent stars of the fashion scene. Although his creations are sold all over the world, he remains loyal to his Flemish homeland. Of the group known as the Antwerp Six, six avant-garde Belgian designers who exerted a lasting influence on the eighties fashion scene with their conceptual garments, he has had the most consistent career. But he is respected and esteemed not only for his independence—he does not conform to trends, and from the start he has stood on his own financially—but also for his luxurious fabrics and matchless flair for color.

From the beginning, Dries Van Noten had an un-beatable advantage: he did not so much grow into fashion, but was rather born into it. His grandfather had opened the first ready-to-wear men's shop in Antwerp, his father owned two luxury boutiques, and his mother ran a franchise shop. As a boy he was already accompanying his parents to fashion shows and fairs in Milan, Düsseldorf, and Paris, never imagining that one day people would line up in Paris to see his creations on the catwalk. At the age of eighteen he attended the renowned Royal Academy of Fine Arts in Antwerp and supple-mented his studies in fashion design by working freelance for various labels. In 1986, when Dries had just turned twenty-eight, he already had a label of his own. In the very same year, Van Noten embarked on a legendary journey with five fellow students (Ann Demeulemeester, Martin Margiela (see page 120), Walter van Beirendonck, Dirk van Saene, and Dirk Bikkembergs). Their collective destination was London Fashion Week. "Come and see the six Belgian designers!" their flyer pro-claimed. And the people went. Dries Van Noten's first collection landed straight on the racks of the famous New York store Barneys.

The Antwerp Six struck a nerve of their time. The mood of the mid-eighties was a highly creative one, with London the center. Vivienne Westwood (see page 82) was celebrating her international breakthrough, the British Fashion Council intro-duced an official Fashion Week, John Galliano (see page 132) was causing a furor—something new was always happening. Dries Van Noten was no strident fashion revolutionary, but he did have a distinctive style from the very beginning. "I was impressed because his clothes have an earthy feeling and are very fluid," recalled Barbara Weiser, co-owner of the once legendary Manhattan fashion store Charivari, in 1993. "They're unconventional but they are not weird." Today Dries Van Noten is known above all for uncomplicated, highly wearable designs and very lavish woven or skillfully printed fabrics, often inspired by ethnic styles and manufactured to his specifications. He likes to combine colors and patterns with the same candidness as they appear in nature. This very special mix of quality and originality ensures that creations such as the rose-printed dresses from his debut collection in Paris in 1994, and the famous iris-patterned silk blouse, still possess an air of modernity years later. Another peculiarity of this Belgian is that he does not do what other designers do: he does not advertise, launch perfumes, or design resort collections for wealthy jet-setters; nor does he live in a fashion metropolis, but in a secluded place in the country near Antwerp. Armed with this philosophy and with the help of approximately eighty staff members, by 2009 this reserved Belgian designer had already acquired six flagship stores and some four hundred retail outlets throughout the world. He does not reveal his sales figures. His maxim is: "When you buy Dries Van Noten, you buy an item of clothing, not a label."

1958 Born in Antwerp on May 12
1976–80 Studies fashion at the Academy of Fine Arts in Antwerp
1986 Presents first men's collection and opens first boutique in Antwerp
1987 Presents first women's collection
1989 The flagship store moves to Het Modepalais in Antwerp
1991 Opening of a showroom in Paris
1993 Premiere at the prêt-à-porter shows in Paris
2007 Opening of a boutique in Paris

Dries Van Noten

Runway at a Dries Van Noten show

1900 Derivation of radiation
law by Max Planck

1929 First presentation of the Academy
Awards, known as the Oscars

1957 Launch of the first
artificial earth
satellite, *Sputnik*,
by the Soviet Union

1888 First issue of the *Financial Times*

1913 George Bernard Shaw
publishes *Pygmalion*

1944 Founding of the
International
Monetary Fund

| 1880 | 1885 | 1890 | 1895 | 1900 | 1905 | 1910 | 1915 | 1920 | 1925 | 1930 | 1935 | 1940 | 1945 | 1950 | 1955 | 1960 | 1965 |

Dress from the spring/summer 2009
collection

1971 The Starbucks Corporation
is founded

1990 End of the Cold War declared by 34 nations of
the Conference on Security and Co-operation

1982 Falklands War

2004 Eastern expansion of the EU

1970 · 1975 · 1980 · 1985 · 1990 · 1995 · 2000 · 2005 · 2010 · 2015 · 2020 · 2025 · 2030 · 2035 · 2040 · 2045 · 2050 · 2055

DOLCE & GABBANA

Sensuality and sex appeal are the trademarks of this designer duo. Creations such as the corset dress made them the international spokesmen for Italian diva fashion.

"Vere Donne" (real women) was the title of the first collection presented by Domenico Dolce and Stefano Gabbana in Milan in 1986. Two words which were to become an enduring credo. Erotic, dramatic, eccentric: Dolce & Gabbana still produce fashion for the archetype of the Italian diva.

The creative power of this designer duo is deeply rooted in their Italian homeland. It is inspired by the neo-realist films of Fellini, Rossellini, and Visconti. And by Sicily. The suits of the *mafiosi*, the girls' traditional black dresses with peasant skirt, fringed shawl, and lace, the mixture of feminine and masculine, delicate and tough, aristocracy and proletariat—all an ode to the Mediterranean island. This was where Domenico Dolce grew up in the sixties, the son of a clothing manufacturer. At eighteen, the boy left home and moved to the North Italian metropolis. There he met Stefano Gabbana, an accomplished graphic designer, and taught him his tailoring skills. They became partners, both professionally and privately.

It all began with small collections shown on a few models in their studio. This soon changed. They were in the right place: Milan and its mighty designers Giorgio Armani (see page 60), Gianni Versace (see page 96), and Gianfranco Ferré were attracting the attention of international fashion. But instead of matching the discreet elegance of the trendsetter Armani, they did exactly the opposite—they created curvy corset dresses, sharply cut pinstripe suits, and tight-fitting leopard-print coats. Conspicuous sex appeal became their trademark. "The first piece of theirs I wore was a white shirt, very chaste, but cut to make my breasts look as if they were bursting out of it," their muse Isabella Rossellini later recalled. The secret of these two designers is that every ordinary woman wearing their creations becomes a celebrated star. The stage and the blaze of flash-bulbs are Dolce & Gabbana's home. For these designers like to celebrate not only their clothes but also themselves—they have produced no fewer than eight books about themselves, and regularly stage huge parties in their own honor.

Success is proving them right: in 2009 their organization employed nearly 4,000 staff members worldwide. The *New York Times* highlighted the achievements of Domenico Dolce and Stefano Gabbana in an article marking their twenty-year anniversary: "It does not seem likely that many people could have envisioned a way to turn distressed jeans or sluttish corsets or pointy-toed shoes or slick suits or football jerseys into an irresistible global export. Yet Mr. Dolce and Mr. Gabbana did."

1958 Domenico Dolce born in Polizzi Generosa, Italy, on August 13

1962 Stefano Gabbana born in Milan on November 14

BEFORE 1980 Domenico Dolce studies fashion design, Stefano Gabbana graphic design

1980 The designers meet in a Milan studio, where both are working as assistants

1982 They begin their joint career with their first designs for Italian fashion producers and the sale of their own models in Milan boutiques

1986 Joint founding of a fashion business and presentation of their first women's collection

1990 First men's collection

1992 Launch of their first perfume, Dolce & Gabbana

2006 Co-branding between Dolce & Gabbana and Motorola to market editions of the Motorola RAZR cell phone

left
Look from the fall/winter 2008/2009 collection

above
Stefano Dolce and Domenico Gabbana, 2007

left
Dress from the spring/summer
2008 collection

right page
Look of the fall/winter 2003/04
collection

1902 Cuba wins independence from Spain

1936–39 Spanish Civil War

1956–59 Construction of th
Guggenheim Museum
New York, designed b
Frank Lloyd Wright

1891–1916 Construction of the
Trans-Siberian Railway

1921 Albert Einstein receives the
Nobel Prize for Physics

1948 Assassination of Mahatma Gandhi

| 1880 | 1885 | 1890 | 1895 | 1900 | 1905 | 1910 | 1915 | 1920 | 1925 | 1930 | 1935 | 1940 | 1945 | 1950 | 1955 | 1960 | 1965 |

Look from the spring/summer 2008
prêt-à-porter collection

1975 Beginning of the Pol Pot
regime in Cambodia

1982 Michael Jackson releases the
album *Thriller*

1992–95 Bosnian War

2002 Introduction of the Euro

1970 1975 1980 1985 1990 1995 2000 2005 2010 2015 2020 2025 2030 2035 2040 2045 2050 2055

JOHN GALLIANO

The costume designer among couturiers combines historical inspiration with modern influences in a masterly fashion.

At first glance it seems unusual for, of all people, John Galliano, whose creative roots lie in London's subversive street style, to have been entrusted with the creative direction of the traditional house of Dior. At second glance, perhaps not—no one avails himself more freely of fashion's historical wealth than this spectacular British fashion fantasist. Galliano's creations may be extravagant, but the craftsmanship behind them is well grounded in tradition. No wonder, for his knowledge of style and cut is considered masterly.

John Galliano was born in Gibraltar and grew up in England, where his Spanish mother wasted neither opportunity nor expense in dressing him up. His graduation show, "Les Incroyables," at London's Central St. Martins in 1984, was influenced by the eccentric style of the French Revolution-era dandies and took the fashion world by storm. In an unprecedented move, one of the most influential London fashion boutiques, Browns, dedicated an entire window display to the young graduate. "Les Incroyables" set the trend for Galliano's style, which has forever remained the same: theatrical, wildly romantic, and of superior quality.
In the years that followed, the then up-and-coming designer showed a series of impressive collections at London Fashion Week. Always ready with a wealth of historical and cultural allusions, for each collection he chose a particular theme, among them "The Ludic Game," "Fallen Angels," and "Forgotten Innocents." Among insiders, Galliano's early pieces were highly valued, but commercial success did not follow. His creations were considered eccentric and unwearable—and yet in the end they allowed their creator to establish himself in Paris in the early nineties.
It was not only his romantic leanings that attracted Galliano to Paris; after all, it was here that an international clientele and fashion press were to be found. In 1993, with the help of the influential editor

of American *Vogue*, Anna Wintour, he found investors and was able to make his fashion accessible to a broad public. This was his breakthrough.
In 1995, as newly appointed chief designer, he dusted off the Givenchy label, and two years later, he moved, within the LVMH group, to become creative director of Dior. There he not only revitalized the artistic legacy of the label's founder, but his themed shows, which soon became legendary, gave fresh creative energy to the whole fashion industry (invitations to the sought-after events were disguised as love letters, hung on rusty keys, or concealed as wrist bands inside Russian dolls).
A citizen of the world, Galliano shows, with a consistency that never grows old, how new ideas can find their natural place in the multilayered history of style. And yet, he views his achievements in considerably more modest terms. In the end, he sees himself as merely "an accomplice to helping women get what they want."

1960 Born in Gibraltar on November 28
1984 Graduates from Central
St. Martins College for Art and
Design in London and becomes an
independent fashion designer
1985 Presents his first collection
1986–89 Peder Bertelsen, a Danish
entrepreneur, invests in the label
1987–89 Responsible for the prêt-à-porter collections at the house
of Balenciaga
1991 Moves studio from London to
Paris; costume design for Kylie
Minogue's "Let's Get to It" tour
1995–96 Chief designer at house of
Givenchy
SINCE 1996 Chief designer at house
of Dior
2008 Launch of first perfume,
John Galliano

above
John Galliano, 2007

following pages
left
Gown inspired by Marie Antoinette from
the Christian Dior fall/winter 2000/01
haute couture collection

right
Pirate look from the spring/summer 2008
collection

1895 Wilhelm Conrad Roentgen
discovers X-rays

1923 First issue of *Time* magazine

1949 Founding of NATO

1911 Founding of the artists' group
Der Blaue Reiter in Munich

1938 Discovery of atomic fission by
Otto Hahn and Fritz Strassmann

1962 Premiere
the first J
Bond film
Dr. No

1880　1885　1890　1895　1900　1905　1910　1915　1920　1925　1930　1935　1940　1945　1950　1955　1960　1965

1978 The Galápagos Islands become the
first UNESCO World Heritage site

2001 George W. Bush becomes
43rd U.S. president

1991 Beginning of the
Balkan conflict

2008 Kosovo declares independence
from Serbia

| 1970 | 1975 | 1980 | 1985 | 1990 | 1995 | 2000 | 2005 | 2010 | 2015 | 2020 | 2025 | 2030 | 2035 | 2040 | 2045 | 2050 | 2055 |

TOM FORD

The "King of Cool" became known for his successful re-launch of the Italian house of Gucci. His own label combines tradition, modern design, and absolute exclusivity.

"Designers sell a perfect world," said Tom Ford in an interview, "A world in which our clients do not need to think, because everything has been thought about already." Tom Ford is a perfectionist down to the cuff of the pristine white shirt peaking from the sleeve of his velvet jacket. *Vogue* editor in chief Anna Wintour disclosed that at dinner parties he matches the colors of the vegetables with the table decoration. Only someone like Tom Ford could achieve what he did in the nineties—transform a dusty label into a coveted symbol of pure luxury: Gucci. The Texan restored the leather-goods company founded in 1921 in Florence to the glamorous heights it had reached in the sixties, when Jackie Kennedy descended from an airplane with a Gucci bag over her shoulder. And he converted the brand into a universe of goods ranging from fashion to high heels, from yoga mats to guitars. In the mid-nineties he attracted stars by the dozens with his fabulous creations—a floor-length white tube dress with a silver clasp at the waist, or a midnight blue ensemble of flared velvet trousers and unbuttoned silk blouse. And he managed to convince women to spend a month's salary every season on a purse. With creations like his "Horsebit bag" adorned with stylized snaffles, the "must-have" phenomenon was born. In the spring of 2004, when Tom Ford presented his final Gucci collection, bidding farewell with the song "Free (To Do What You Want To Do)" and with a homage to himself, the whole fashion industry went into mourning for its "King of Cool," the man who transformed the nineties into the decade of glamour. His legacy in figures: increasing Gucci's revenues from 230 million to almost three billion dollars.

This success proves that Tom Ford is not only a designer of genius, but also an accomplished marketing strategist. His American roots are often given the credit for his talent. Hailing from Austin, Texas, in the early eighties Tom Ford studied at the legendary Parsons School of Design in both New York and Paris. He was not even thirty when he first joined Gucci as a womenswear designer. Four years later he was creative director, and six years after that, when the Gucci Group took over Yves Saint Laurent, he was in charge of both fashion houses. The designer is said to sleep little, but when he does, always with Post-it notes by his pillow, in case a good idea strikes in the night.

Since his departure from Gucci, the new chapter in Tom Ford's success story is called "Tom Ford." Bearing his name are perfumes, cosmetics, sunglasses, and a highly exclusive men's collection that replaced Brioni as the traditional outfitter for James Bond. In the continually expanding empire of Tom Ford stores, the designer takes luxury to the limit, even further than he had with Gucci and Yves Saint Laurent. In a perfectly staged residential environment with a butler, maids, and a custom tailoring service, Ford aspires to unite tradition, first-class quality, and modern design in an elite shop concept. He almost completely rejects the seasonal collection calendar and holds no sales. His specialty is classic jackets of specially developed wool-silk or wool-cashmere blends—jackets the handsome designer himself likes to wear.

1961 Born in Austin, Texas,
on August 27
1979–86 Studies art history and
drama, without graduating, and
graduates from Parsons School of
Design, where he studies interior
design
1986–90 Assistant to Cathy Hardwick
and Perry Ellis
1990 Joins Gucci as fashion designer
1994–2004 Creative director at Gucci
1999–2004 Creative director of YSL's
prêt-à-porter collection after
the takeover of the Yves Saint
Laurent label by Gucci
2005 Founds his own label
2006 Launches a range of perfumes,
Tom Ford Beauty
2007 Opens his first flagship store in
New York
2008 Directs the film *A Single Man*

left page
Creations by Tom Ford

above
Tom Ford

1887 First creation of artificial electromagnetic waves by Heinrich Hertz

1909 First Giro d'Italia

1932 Aldous Huxley publishes
Brave New World

1954–62 Algerian War

1897 Tate Gallery opened in London

1921 Ireland wins independence
from the United Kingdom

1944 Founding of the International Bank for
Reconstruction and Development

| 1880 | 1885 | 1890 | 1895 | 1900 | 1905 | 1910 | 1915 | 1920 | 1925 | 1930 | 1935 | 1940 | 1945 | 1950 | 1955 | 1960 | 1965 |

Neon-yellow jacket with exaggerated arms

1970 Forming of the band
Queen

1985 Live Aid charity concert for
famine relief in Africa

1999 The majority of Australians vote in
favor of retaining the monarchy

2006 In Liberia, Ellen Johnson-Sirleaf is
sworn in as the first female African
head of state

1970 1975 1980 1985 1990 1995 2000 2005 2010 2015 2020 2025 2030 2035 2040 2045 2050 2055

MARC JACOBS

An American in Paris: Marc Jacobs is creative director at the traditional house of Louis Vuitton. No less successful is his personal New York–based label.

"I have never again been so sure of anything. I knew that the signs were pointing to change. I sensed the change in the music, knew that beauty in the future will come into being from the imperfect, and I saw Kate Moss, who was beginning to replace the super-models," says Marc Jacobs, the wunderkind of American design, about what was probably the most important day of his career: the one in 1993 when he presented the spring collection for his then employer Perry Ellis. On the catwalk were washed-out shirts in high-quality silk printed with simple lumberjack checks. Then there were creased crepe dresses, combined with horizontally striped sweaters, simple knitted caps, and satin Chuck Taylors. With Jacobs, grunge had arrived to the fashion industry, the last bastion stubbornly clinging to the swaggering style of the eighties. The collection he created at the age of twenty-nine was a sweeping success with the critics—but not the buyers. Perry Ellis was unable to sell a single piece from this collection of supposedly cheap fashion. The company promptly severed ties with its chief designer—until today the most notorious dismissal in the industry. What followed was one of the most successful careers in the contemporary fashion world.

Marc Jacobs was born in New York in 1963, where he grew up with his grandmother, who taught him to knit. As a teenager, what he wanted for Christmas was mainly clothes. At eighteen he began to study at the Parsons School of Design, where as a student he received numerous honors (the greatest of these, if not the most official, was being able to sell his fashions on campus). From 1989 he worked for Perry Ellis, and after his spectacular dismissal he concentrated on his own label, which he founded in 1986 with his business partner Robert Duffy. In 1997 came the highest accolade: the traditional French house of Louis Vuitton appointed the American as its new creative director. Since then, Jacobs has followed his own fashion path on two continents. In New York he works for himself, in Paris for Louis Vuitton. His style is a collage of impressions, feelings, and ideas. His look (for either label) often changes with every collection, yet it clearly shows the signature of its creator. The most obvious trademarks of Jacobs' creations are kitsch-free girlishness, elegant breaches of style, and the skillful integration of kitsch. Particularly with Louis Vuitton, Jacobs likes to turn to extraneous talent from the world of art. The company's legendary brown and beige bags have been recreated in limited editions by, among others, graffiti artist Stephen Sprouse (2000), Japanese artist Takashi Murakami (2003), and Richard Prince (2007).

Marc Jacobs is still the darling of the press. But now, there are also buyers to be found among the ranks of his fans. Marc Jacobs has successfully created his own coveted lines. At Louis Vuitton, which was mainly known before Jacobs' arrival for its production of high-quality luggage, total revenue rose in less than ten years from 940 million to 2.7 billion euros.

1963 Born in New York on April 9
1984 Graduates from Parsons New
School of Design in New York
1986 Presents his first collection
1989–93 Chief designer at Perry Ellis
1996 Introduces a men's collection
SINCE 1997 Chief designer at the
French fashion house of Louis
Vuitton
2000 Launch of the Marc collection
by Marc Jacobs

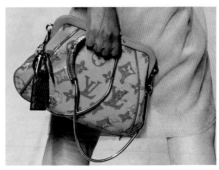

left
Louis Vuitton bag

above
Marc Jacobs, 2009

above
Presentation of the Louis Vuitton
bag collection, 2007

right page
Creations from the fall/winter
2006/07 prêt-à-porter collection

DAVID BOWIE

1901 Theodore Roosevelt becomes
26th U.S. president

1923 Sigmund Freud publishes
The Ego and the Id

1949 People's Republic of China
founded by Mao Zedong

1962 Cuban
Missile
Crisis

1887 Emil Berliner invents the gramophone
and records

1910–29 Mexican Revolution

1939–45 World War II

1880 1885 1890 1895 1900 1905 1910 1915 1920 1925 1930 1935 1940 1945 1950 1955 1960 1965

Slim-cut suit from the spring/summer 2006
collection

1995 Launch of the Japanese electronic
toy Tamagotchi

1979 Islamic Revolution in Iran under the
leadership of the Ayatollah Khomeini

2005 Hurricane Katrina causes massive
flooding in New Orleans

1970 1975 1980 1985 1990 1995 2000 2005 2010 2015 2020 2025 2030 2035 2040 2045 2050 2055

HEDI SLIMANE

With slender silhouettes and a clean aesthetic, the Dior designer became a leading figure in men's fashion.

For ten years the introverted Frenchman stood in the fashion spotlight (three as the director of men's fashions at Yves Saint Laurent, the remaining seven as creative director at Dior Homme). Over that period he is reputed to have defined the look of the new millennium, even having reinvented men's fashion. Then, in the spring of 2007, Hedi Slimane bade a premature farewell to the world's catwalks. A Paris newspaper summed up the feelings of grief in the fashion world: "God has gone." The fashion designer, however, had never wished to make a grand entrance.

As a child, the son of an Italian mother and Tunisian father, he was an outsider who adopted the role of an observer. From his mother, who made the family's clothing, he acquired a basic knowledge of sewing. In 1996, after studying art history and an apprenticeship in couture with José Lévy, the as yet unknown twenty-eight-year-old attracted the attention of Yves Saint Laurent (see page 64), the icon of haute couture. Slimane became chief designer of Saint Laurent's men's line, and within three years he was a fashion superstar. His drain-pipe jeans, tight jackets, and slim-fitting suits were the clothing of a new generation. The former out-sider had made excellent use of his extraordinary talent for observation: his early collections demonstrate not only his unassailable taste, but also an already almost clairvoyant sense of what was to come.

His move to Dior was followed by the first scandal of the new millennium. And it was not because Slimane changed employers; his refusal to work under the American Tom Ford (see page 136) after the Gucci Group's takeover of YSL was even seen by the French press as a patriotic act. It was the presentation of his first Dior collection that caused a furor. There applauding from the front row was none other than Yves Saint Laurent, his former mentor, in person.

At least as exciting: his fashion. The suits, shirts, trousers, and sweaters had such a ruthlessly slim silhouette that they failed to match the old masculine ideal (tall, athletic, muscular). At Dior, Slimane held fast to the new slender artist's look he had introduced. He dressed musicians such as Pete Doherty, Beck, Mick Jagger, The Libertines, and Franz Ferdinand, and, in a well-publicized move, Karl Lagerfeld (see page 70) lost ninety pounds just to be able to wear Slimane's Dior jeans.

Slimane largely rejected the use of patterns in his designs. His color palette ranged mainly from black to white. His cutting was precise and followed the rules of classic couture even though he constantly reinterpreted them. Fashion for Slimane was more than an attractive cloth wrapping. It was the visible now, a reflection of the moment. For precisely that reason, Slimane did not hire his models (mostly skinny teenagers) from agencies, but directly from the streets of Berlin, London, and New York. They demonstrated what Slimane's fashion represented. It was the quest for an uncomplicated life, the creative process of imperfection: "Everything always revolves around this moment of being young, the enormous energy that lies in it, and this idea that anything is possible. This has nothing to do with nostalgia, after all the work is not about me. I am a total observer here, not someone who is in mourning for his own youth. That has already been lost, as can be seen."

When Slimane left the house of Dior after contract negotiations failed, the mourning was one-sided. For the Frenchman, who even during his time as a fashion designer felt at home in diverse creative fields (above all photography), the medium is of secondary importance. "The only thing that is important," says Hedi Slimane, "is the idea."

1968 Born in Paris on July 5
1992–95 Works with José Lévy
1996–99 Chief designer of men's
collection for Yves Saint Laurent
2000–7 Chief designer of men's
collection for Christian Dior
2002 Publication of first photography
book, *Intermission 1*
2007 Curates first exhibition, *Sweet
Bird of Youth*

Hedi Slimane

1890 First inoculation of a human
with immune serum

1919 The treaty of Versailles formally
ends World War I

1949 David Ben Gurion becomes
first prime minister of Israel

1901 First Nobel Prize awarded by the
King of Sweden in Stockholm

1937 Exhibition of "Degenerate Art"
in Munich

1880   1885   1890   1895   1900   1905   1910   1915   1920   1925   1930   1935   1940   1945   1950   1955   1960   1965

Flared red dress from the fall/winter 2009
prêt-à-porter collection

VANESSA BEECROFT

2001 George W. Bush becomes 43rd U.S. president

1979 Saddam Hussein becomes
president of Iraq

2007 The Apple iPhone goes on sale

4–73 Vietnam War

1991 The World Wide Web made
publicly available

1970   1975   1980   1985   1990   1995   2000   2005   2010   2015   2020   2025   2030   2035   2040   2045   2050   2055

ALEXANDER MCQUEEN

Brilliantly crazy: the British "bad boy" polarizes with his razor-sharp tailoring and poetically provocative staging.

"I'm a big anarchist. I don't believe in religion, or in another human being wanting to govern over someone else…. I do believe fashion is a voice." Alexander McQueen's words are nothing less than the manifesto of a designer who from the beginning has used the catwalk as a platform for provocation. Dramatically staged events are the trademark of this London-born designer, whose great skill is evident in his precise, often historically inspired designs. It is no surprise that Alexander McQueen is considered controversial in the fashion business. His mix of the avant-garde, poetry, provocation, and high-quality tailoring elicits the most diverse reactions: at times attacked as a "bad boy," other times hailed as "Alexander the Great." When, at the tender age of twenty-seven, he was appointed head designer of the Paris couture house of Givenchy, the press wrote of him that he was a "punk whom you would rather not meet in the dark." A few years later he received the title of Commander of the British Empire from Queen Elizabeth II.

Alexander McQueen, the son of a taxi driver and the youngest of six children, grew up in the seventies in the working-class East End of London. At an early age he showed a great interest in fashion, to the amusement of his classmates, who called the blond boy with the piercing blue eyes "McQueer." At sixteen, Alexander McQueen left school and began an apprenticeship in Savile Row, the London street renowned for its custom tailoring establishments. His extensive training in classic British traditions still characterizes his style today, and is seen above all in his jackets, precisely cut to the shape of the body. He is a master of six different cutting techniques, from the dramatic forms of the sixteenth century to the sharp-edged couture that is his trademark today. Typical of McQueen's style are his edgy, almost aggressive cuts and silhouettes. When he received his master's degree in 1994 from the renowned Central St. Martin's College of Art and

Design in London, he entered the public eye for the first time: the British fashion journalist and icon Isabella Blow had bought his entire graduation collection, allegedly for £5,000. The following year he presented his, in many respects standard-setting, Highland Rape collection. He introduced his famous low-cut "bumster" pants, and, with his torn garments and blood-smeared models, established himself as a designer with a tendency towards gloomy drama. Apart from his perfect cuts and wayward poetry, provocation is his most important stylistic device. His catwalk shows have featured wolves, and models encircled by flames or soaked with rain. Alexander McQueen also hit the headlines in 1999 when he presented the Paralympic sprinter Aimee Mullins as a model on his catwalk. She appeared before the international fashion press walking on hand-carved wooden legs.

In spite of the scandals, it was he and his eccentric compatriot John Galliano (see page 132) who, in the tradition of Thierry Mugler (see page 102) and Jean Paul Gaultier (see page 114), gave a new impetus to the Paris fashion scene of the nineties. Within a few years Alexander McQueen was awarded all the important international fashion prizes. Since moving his runway shows from London to Paris in 2001, he has become firmly established in the French metropolis. He owns several flagship stores worldwide, and every season he successfully conserves his reputation as a brilliant rebel.

1969 Born in London on March 17
FROM 1985 Tailoring apprenticeship at Anderson and Sheppard and Gieves and Hawkes on Savile Row, London
1992–94 Assistant at Romeo Gigli in Milan
1992 Founds the Alexander McQueen label
1994 Graduates from Central St. Martins College for Art & Design in London
1996–2001 Chief designer at house of Givenchy in Paris
2000 51% of the label goes to Gucci, where Alexander McQueen is still creative director
2002 Opening of the first flagship store in New York
2003 Receives the CFDA Award as International Designer of the Year

Alexander McQueen, 2003

left page
Presentation of the spring/summer
collection

below
Spring/summer 2010 prêt-à-porter
collection

1886 The Statue of Liberty constructed
in New York Harbor

1915–17 Armenian Genocide
in the Ottoman Empire

1940 The first McDonald's
restaurant opens

1956 Elvis Presley releases
"Heartbreak Hotel,"
his first big hit

1903–4 British expedition to Tibet

1924 First performance of George Gershwin's
Rhapsody in Blue

1880 1885 1890 1895 1900 1905 1910 1915 1920 1925 1930 1935 1940 1945 1950 1955 1960 1965

From Fashion and Back exhibition
at the Design Museum, London, 2009

1969 Jonathan Beckwith is the first to successfully isolate a single gene

1980–88 Iran-Iraq War

1991 Boris Yeltsin becomes first democratically elected president of Russia

2003 Completion of mapping of the human genome

1970 1975 1980 1985 1990 1995 2000 2005 2010 2015 2020 2025 2030 2035 2040 2045 2050 2055

HUSSEIN CHALAYAN

Chalayan is the conceptual artist among fashion designers. His collections are influenced by politics, technology, and current events.

"In my world it's a question of the present, about life as it is now. How power is used and abused. I think about the importance of nations and states, and about how we are influenced by history—in my work I react to all these things." Anyone unfamiliar with Hussein Chalayan could not imagine this was a fashion designer speaking. And in fact he is rather different than most of those who work full-time creating fashion.

With his graduate collection "Buried" at St. Martins College of Art and Design in London in 1993, Chalayan was already proving that he was far more than a competent couturier. He buried his creations—silk dresses covered with iron filings—underground and left them for weeks. The idea was that the clay-encrusted, semi-decomposed dresses would make patent the process of decay. The show, which was meant to represent the transience of life, was a resounding success. Chalayan won the Absolut Design Award, and the collection was sold in the exclusive London boutique Browns. The prize money helped Chalayan finance his debut in London Fashion Week (it is only since 2001 that he has been showing in Paris). What had already become evident during his studies was confirmed in his first independent show: Chalayan is the brilliant conceptual artist of the fashion industry.

His collections are oriented less toward aesthetics or seasonal trends than toward themes of his own choosing. His artistic approach is supported by a sophisticated use of technology. In presentations less reminiscent of conventional fashion shows than of modern stage productions or avant-garde

free-space installations, Chalayan uses fashion to take on the topics that interest him, principally cultural and social conflicts. Two of his collections—"Between" (1998) and "Kinship Journeys" (2003)—explored the significance and position of Islamic culture. In his presentation, Chalayan showed models wearing the traditional chador, some completely covered, some naked except for a headscarf. In the much-discussed collection "Afterwords" (2001), he addressed artistically the precarious reality of refugees. The catwalk was a staged living room, with furniture on which Chalayan presented his fashions. At the end of the show, the models pulled the covers off the sofas and dressed themselves in the upholstery. The framework of the furniture was folded up and carried off the stage as luggage. All that was left was an unremarkable coffee table with a hole in the middle. The last remaining model climbed into it, pulled the table up like a collapsible travel cup, and fastened it to her hip. She left the now empty stage wearing her new skirt.

Even if Chalayan's intellectual fashion is not always wearable, it convinces art and fashion experts equally. Probably no other living designer has been the subject of as many exhibitions as this British citizen with Turkish Cypriot roots. Nevertheless, he

is unlikely to achieve great commercial success. His studio has repeatedly struggled to survive. Since 2008, the sporting goods firm Puma has been the label's majority shareholder. According to Chalayan, this association is intended to bring his fashion to a wider audience.

1970 Born in Nicosia on August 12
1993 Graduates from Central St. Martins College for Art & Design in London
1995 Presents his first collection
1998–2001 Assistant at the New York knitwear label TSE
2002 Presents his first men's collection
2004 Opens his first flagship store in Tokyo
2005 Represents Turkey at the Venice Biennale
SINCE 2008 Creative director of Puma, which acquires a majority share in the Hussein Chalayan label

left
An unusual outfit by Hussein Chalayan: the dress opens automatically. A creation from his spring/summer 2007 collection

above
Hussein Chalayan, 2008

Lit-up hat from the fall/winter 2007/08
prêt-à-porter collection

1905 Russian Revolution

1928 Walt Disney creates the cartoon character Mickey Mouse

1959 Miles Davis releases the album *Kind of Blue*

1894 First performance of Claude Debussy's *Prélude à l'après-midi d'un faune*

1918–20 Worldwide influenza epidemic claims the lives of more than 20 million people

1943 First New York Fashion Week

1880 1885 1890 1895 1900 1905 1910 1915 1920 1925 1930 1935 1940 1945 1950 1955 1960 1965

Puff-sleeved dress with deep décolleté

1976 Helmut Newton publishes his first
photography book, *White Women*

2004 Founding of the online
social network Facebook

1992 The Maastricht Treaty results in the
founding of the European Union (EU)

| 1970 | 1975 | 1980 | 1985 | 1990 | 1995 | 2000 | 2005 | 2010 | 2015 | 2020 | 2025 | 2030 | 2035 | 2040 | 2045 | 2050 | 2055 |

STELLA MCCARTNEY

She designs fashion without leather, campaigns for animals, and lives on a strict vegan diet. No other designer combines high-end fashion with a green conscience as consistently as Stella McCartney.

Sometimes a single piece of news is enough to throw the whole fashion world off kilter. When Paris fashion house Chloé announced in 1997 that it was replacing its chief designer with the barely twenty-five-year-old newcomer Stella McCartney, a veritable storm of indignation broke out. Most of the fashion press regarded the appointment of the young daughter of a Beatle as a last desperate attempt of the label, at that time decidedly passé (their previous two collections were met with jeers), to at least capitalize on her famous name. Karl Lagerfeld (see page 70), himself a former couturier at Chloé and not exactly squeamish about berating his colleagues, was unsparing in his derision. Of course he desired a big name for Chloé—but from the world of fashion, not music; one could only hope that the daughter was as talented as the father. Lagerfeld's wish, though ironic, was to be fulfilled. McCartney not only led Chloé into the new millennium, but within a short time she vastly increased sales. Above all, however, she catapulted the Paris label to exactly the position it had occupied in the seventies: in the league of the most coveted brands.

A lot has changed since her debut at Chloé. Now, in cooperation with Gucci, Stella McCartney runs her own label whose fashions are sold in more than fifty countries. And with every new collection she liberates herself a bit more from the image of a daughter of rock royalty. Stories such as the one about her graduation fashion show at the renowned Central St. Martins College of Art in London are slowly fading away. At that time, she had her friends Kate Moss, Naomi Campbell, and Yasmin LeBon treading her catwalk, to great public acclaim, while Twiggy and McCartney's parents, Linda and Paul, applauded from the front row. But even as a student, the young British designer, who completed her first apprenticeship with Christian Lacroix (see page 112) at only fifteen, already had more to offer than a famous name. She had talent and, more importantly, a virtuoso style of her own. The distinctive look of Stella McCartney is a mixture of feminine neo-romanticism and urbane functional modernity. Flowing fabrics in pastel shades, delicate lace and sweet puffed sleeves are matched with perfectly tailored, slightly masculine cuts, which can be seen as a tribute to her apprenticeship on London's Savile Row, famous for its traditional men's bespoke tailoring. But there is one thing missing in McCartney's designs, whether in her own line or her sport collection for Adidas: leather, not to mention fur. Even if she could substantially increase her sales, as she herself suspects, McCartney refuses to countenance the killing of animals for something as trivial as fashion. A mother of three, she lives a vegan lifestyle (just like her parents, who inevitably always seem to come up), uses wind power as an energy source for her flagship stores, and provides shopping bags of re-cycled paper.

Looking at the designer's steep upward career trajectory one cannot quite shake off the impression that she has used her name to open doors. It may just be, however, that she has made her own way. Her strength does not lie in her background, but in her consistency. Not only the consistency of her convictions, but above all of her incredibly personal style that, despite all prejudices, she is able to preserve.

1971 Born in London on September 13
1995 Graduates from St. Martins College for Art & Design in London
1997–2001 Chief designer for the Paris fashion house Chloé
2001 Founds the Stella McCartney label and presents her first collection
2003 Launches her first perfume, Stella
2004 Costumes for Madonna's "Re-Invention" tour
2006 Spring/summer collection with prints by Jeff Koons
2007 100%-organic cosmetic line Care with Yves Saint Laurent

Stella McCartney, 2009

HAUTE COUTURE, PRÊT-À-PORTER, CONFECTION

Fashion design today is divided into three categories: haute couture, prêt-à-porter, and confection. At the top are the exclusive, made-to-measure creations of haute couture, high-class tailoring. For a fashion label to be allowed to officially describe itself as a couture house, it must present at least thirty-five new models every season (for both day and evening wear), which must have been manufactured by at least fifteen full-time staff members in a proprietary studio in Paris. Haute couture models for private clients must be made to measure after at least one personal fitting. Adherence to these criteria, laid down and protected by the French state, is annually checked by the French Chamber of Commerce. Also to be seen at the fashion weeks are prêt-à-porter collections. In contrast to haute couture, the models are not made to measure, but produced in standardized sizes. And although they generally dispense with luxury details such as St. Gallen lace and hand-sewn pearls, prêt-à-porter models are distinguished by high quality, unusual details, and precision cutting. They, more often than haute couture, are the source of inspiration for everyday fashion, which is generally retailed under the name of confection. The latter is manufactured in large quantities by mass-production methods from ready-made model designs.

INDEX

Alaïa, Azzedine 80
Armani, Giorgio 60

Balenciaga, Cristóbal 28
Balmain, Pierre 38

Chalayan, Hussein 148
Chanel, Gabrielle "Coco" 20
Confection 155
Courrèges, André 44

De la Renta, Oscar 50
Dior, Christian 30
Dolce & Gabbana 128

Ford, Tom 136

Galliano, John 132
Garavani, Valentino 52
Gaultier, Jean Paul 114
Givenchy, Hubert de 46

Halston, Roy 48
Haute Couture 155

Jacobs, Marc 138

Karan, Donna 104
Kawakubo, Rei 90
Klein, Calvin 86

Lacroix, Christian 112
Lagerfeld, Karl 70
Lang, Helmut 118
Lanvin, Jeanne 12
Lauren, Ralph 74

Main Bocher 24
Margiela, Martin 120
McCartney, Stella 152
McQueen, Alexander 144
Missoni 40
Miyake, Issey 68
Moschino, Franco 110
Mugler, Thierry 102

Poiret, Paul 16
Prada, Miuccia 106
Prêt-à-Porter 155
Pucci, Emilio 34

Quant, Mary 58

Ricci, Nina 18

Sander, Jil 94
Saint Laurent, Yves 64
Schiaparelli, Elsa 26
Slimane, Hedi 142
Takada, Kenzo 76

Ungaro, Emanuel 56

Van Noten, Dries 124
Versace, Gianni 96
Vionnet, Madeleine 14
Von Furstenberg, Diane 100

Westwood, Vivienne 82

Yamamoto, Yohji 92

PHOTO CREDITS